Your Towns and Cities in the

Colchester
in the Great War

Your Towns and Cities in the Great War

Colchester
in the Great War

Andrew Phillips

Pen & Sword
MILITARY

First published in Great Britain in 2017 by
PEN & SWORD MILITARY
an imprint of
Pen and Sword Books Ltd
47 Church Street
Barnsley
South Yorkshire S70 2AS

ISBN 978 1 47386 061 2

Printed and bound in England
by CPI Group (UK) Ltd, Croydon, CR0 4YY

Typeset in Times New Roman by Chic Graphics

Pen & Sword Books Ltd incorporates the imprints of
Pen & Sword Archaeology, Atlas, Aviation, Battleground, Discovery,
Family History, History, Maritime, Military, Naval, Politics, Railways,
Select, Social History, Transport, True Crime, Claymore Press,
Frontline Books, Leo Cooper, Praetorian Press, Remember When,
Seaforth Publishing and Wharncliffe.

For a complete list of Pen and Sword titles please contact
Pen and Sword Books Limited
47 Church Street, Barnsley, South Yorkshire, S70 2AS, England
E-mail: enquiries@pen-and-sword.co.uk
Website: www.pen-and-sword.co.uk

Contents

Acknowledgements

I would like to acknowledge, in alphabetical order, the help I have received with illustrations and information from Robert Beaken, Paul Byrne, Patrick Denney, Norman Jacobs, Jess Jephcott, Heather Johnson, Paul Rusiecki and Steve Yates.

The sources for this book are the contemporary press, the Colchester Recalled oral history archive, material housed at the Essex Record Office and material published by other Colchester historians.

Measurements
In 1914–18 one pound in weight equalled 16 ounces. One pound in money (£) equalled 20 shillings. One foot in length was equal to .305 metres.

Andrew Phillips, March 2016

CHAPTER 1

Colchester in 1914

Colchester in 1914 was bustling and prosperous. Unemployment scarcely existed. In just thirty years this economically stagnant market town had been transformed by the growth of modern industry. Factories had been built for engineering, printing and the mass production of men's clothing, and modern plant for milling and brewing. This boosted a flourishing service sector of pubs, shops and professional services. It also stimulated building: houses were going up everywhere. Paradoxically this success was helped by the depressed state of Essex

Bustling and prosperous.' The view of Colchester's Head Street from the top of a tram.

Within 10 miles of Colchester rural poverty was widespread. The poster on the wall of the house advertises the 1909 Pageant.

agriculture, the town's historic constituency. Rural incomes were desperately low, enabling Colchester to pay wages below those of economic rivals in London or the industrial north.

Colchester's clothing factories, for example, employed an army of women outworkers in villages up to a ten-mile radius from the town, paying piece rates which were routinely denounced as 'sweated'. These modest earnings boosted household incomes otherwise barely sustained by the husband's agricultural wages. Similarly, unskilled labourers readily accepted the wages offered by the town's engineering firms since they were better than farm wages. A further economic asset was Colchester's colourful port, the Hythe. Railways were the mass transport of the age, bringing manufactured goods to stock Colchester's shops, as well as the raw materials, above all coal, to power Colchester's economy. But, if railway freight costs rose, Colchester merchants might use the river instead. Thus the Hythe, open to cargo ships at high tide, had become the town's industrial heart. The rail link to the Hythe's quays gave local industry instant access to both river and rail. Paxman's, the engineering firm on Hythe Hill, got pig iron, coal and coke by both railway and river, persuading the railway to build special rolling stock to carry their giant boilers from a railhead at the Hythe to anywhere in Britain, including the Port of London for export overseas.

Colchester's economic growth boosted the town's rateable value, financing a spectacular rise in the role of local government, as the town council invested extensively in facilities and infrastructure. Since 1880 they had built and sustained a public library, the Castle Park, the Old Heath Recreation Ground, a museum, a twenty-four-hour water supply via a water tower nicknamed Jumbo, a sewage system, a fire brigade, regular refuse collections, eight newly-built council schools, a school of art and a technical school, governance of the Royal Grammar School, an electricity supply system, a tramway network, improved river dredging, new quays at the Hythe, a profitable oyster fishery, a police force, four bridges and 80 miles of road. During 1914 Colchester Borough Council and its committees held over 800 meetings. There had been nothing like this before. And Colchester was now well run, a major advantage in the turmoil which lay ahead.

Mayor Wilson Marriage welcomes his guests to the new town hall.

The council was a major employer too. Its empire was run from a new town hall, opened in 1903 in the centre of High Street, a lavish, flamboyant statement of civic power. To be a town councillor was to be a leading light, but you had to get elected; to be an alderman was reserved for city fathers, senior political figures and often masters of large businesses in the town. Corporate Colchester was male and proud: proud of its history, proud of its independence. Though Westminster and Chelmsford, home of Essex County Council, were facts of life, Colchester, these men felt, could run itself. However, the decision in 1913 to grant Chelmsford the cathedral for which Colchester had also bid was a civic setback.

Colchester High Street followed a line laid down by the Romans in AD 43 and was the centre of the town. Every Saturday it housed a market: a long line of stalls selling everything, trading late into the

A military band plays in the Castle Park bandstand, part of the recreational infrastructure the Council had established.

Colchester's broad High Street, dominated by the town hall, a car, a bicycle and, far left, a steam wagon.

night, lit by naphtha flares. Around it central Colchester was full of shops, most locally owned. Only four were branches of national chains. Not till 1914 did Woolworth's, the best known of them, arrive.

Child Labour

Ethel Appleby, born 1901

I left school at 12 and went straight into domestic service. We had to start at six in the morning lighting the kitchen fire, cleaning the grate, doing the steps, cleaning the brass, cleaning the windows, washing up and helping with the clothes washing. We worked all day. In the afternoon there would be sewing or ironing to do and then it would be time to get the tea ready. When that was finished, I'd have to clear away and wash up, and then get the hot water bottles ready for the beds, and turn the beds down. After that I'd probably have a few minutes for myself and would perhaps read a book or do some sewing before it would be time to get the supper ready. When that was over it was time for bed.

Jack Ashton, born 1902

*We used to earn a copper or two by what we used to call
'Holding your horse, Sir', because all these farmers and people
who wanted to come into Head Street or High Street to the bank
had to come in by horse and cart, or on horseback, but they
wanted someone to hold the horse while they went into the bank.*

Beyond the town centre lay the suburbs, each a world apart; to cross
from one to the other in 1914 could be to enter a foreign land. Leafy
Lexden Road was Colchester's affluent west end, with architect-
designed mansions, trees from Bunting's Nursery, a cook, a housemaid
and a gardener, and tennis played in whites at the Cambridge Road
Club. South east of High Street lay New Town, home to the upwardly
mobile and the better-paid staff at Paxman's engineering works; full
of young families who went for long walks on Sunday. Privet hedges,
lace curtains and respectability abounded. Church and chapel played a
big part in people's lives and Sunday was a day of rest. True, trams
rumbled into town, army bands played in Castle Park, but football on
the Recreation Ground was frowned on.

 Up by North Station was a community of railway workers. This
merged imperceptibly with 'The North', a largely working class area
in shouting distance of the Cattle Market at Middleborough and
embracing the aging properties now called the Dutch Quarter. Despite

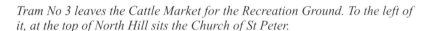

*Tram No 3 leaves the Cattle Market for the Recreation Ground. To the left of
it, at the top of North Hill sits the Church of St Peter.*

The earliest surviving photo (1921) of the all-conquering Barrack Street School football team.

the emerging North Gang, more terrifying for their self-image than their threat to law and order, honest neighbourliness was widespread. Graduates of North School, the borough's first council school, cherished memories of football contests against the hard boys of Barrack Street, the borough's largest school, serving the Hythe district and later re-named the Wilson Marriage School, after the great man, the Quaker miller, who was mayor of Colchester in 1914.

And the countryside, teeming with butterflies, horse flies and wildflowers, was never far away. Many roads were still compacted earth, but bicycles were everywhere and the number of cars and lorries grew daily. As 1914 dawned plans to cover town centre roads with wooden blocks set in pitch were being discussed.

And what did Colchester do? Men worked; women cooked, kept house and raised children. Labour saving devices were few. Children still largely did as they were told, particularly at school, where the cane was widely used, often on both sexes. Jobs were gendered too and a reflection of class. Though the chief objective of women was deemed to be marriage, before that young women worked. Middle-class women worked in offices, where typewriters had arrived: small, dim offices, all floorboards and small carpets, many still lit by gas. Early each morning older, poorer women scrubbed, dusted and lit coal fires before the staff arrived.

Some 250 Colchester women were teachers: in private schools, in council schools. Though shops were owned and staffed by men, shop girls were a growing force. They needed courtesy and stamina: you were stood on your feet all day. Food preparation, inns and lodgings kept another 600 women busy, while 350 did exhausting work in laundries. 'They had to let women do it,' one old lady recalled, 'men could not have coped.'

Almost 2,000 women (that's a third of the total) made clothes, mostly men's coats, jackets and trousers, using industrial sewing machines in large factories, often owned by London firms. You had to get used to a needle going through your finger and rats scurrying round

Tailoresses at Hyam's Clothing Factory.

the floor. An equal number, as we have seen, 'did the tailoring' in local villages, either in small workshops or in their own homes, sitting up late into the night. Domestic servants for Colchester were recruited in villages too, warned by the lady of the house to avoid the company of soldiers.

With only 5,800 women in full time employment, most Colchester women were housewives, feeding their husbands, making ends meet, raising large families, often working part-time: cleaning houses, washing clothes, going pea picking. Many suffered the loss of a baby or worried that their man would die, sending them in old age to the workhouse in Popes Lane.

Rag Trade Remembered

Mrs Andrews, born 1902
There was one door for the workers and one for the managers. Well, when I started I just run up the stairs. I didn't care. And we got a new manager. I didn't know him. And this man said to me, 'What you doing up here?' and I said, 'You mind your own business'. Course, I got reported; he found out who I was. But our foreman was mostly on our side. You know what I mean? He was very strict: very strict indeed. But he looked after his girls. And nothing happened.

Mrs Trusty, born 1901
Oh we used to sing all day long! We used to thoroughly enjoy it. We had a little thing on our machines where we used to wind bobbins, and little cards we had to sew into the garments with our number on. And if anyone got the words of a new song we used to write the songs out and stick them there. And we used to sing all the latest songs. And it was lovely to hear everyone singing. It was marvellous really. That's what kept us going.

Apart from doctors, solicitors, their clerks, some managers and a host of small businessmen, manual labour dominated men's work. This shortened lives dramatically, by accidents or merely by wearing men out. Agriculture-related jobs were in breweries, where free beer encouraged alcoholism, or East Mills where flour and dust might do

The Hythe at low water. The vessel far left is a 'stackie'.

your lungs no good, or the Hythe with its malting, where the rich smell of malt mixed with the whiff of the gasworks next door. Here some of the hardest men in Colchester worked twelve hours on and twelve hours off, 365 days a year, shovelling coal into retorts. For this they were well paid, but the Hythe was nevertheless home to visible poverty and dysfunctional families who regularly graced the magistrates' courts.

Equally tough were the labourers carrying a shoulder of timber or a 120lb sack of oilseed from the hold of a barge up a heaving plank to the shore. New recruits were easy to spot from the caked blood on their shirts. Hard skins, like hard hands, came with experience. Hard hats were for wimps, and nowhere in sight. Early in 1914 a fire destroyed the Hythe's nastiest premises, Wombach's, which officially made sausage skins from animal intestines. Actually they rendered dead animals into things you did not want to know about and smelt even worse than the adjacent sewage works in summer, attracting the attention of the borough's appropriately named Inspector of Nuisances.

But the Hythe was a colourful place, packed with brown-sailed barges, manned by a skipper, a boy and a dog, carrying corn from Colchester and 'general goods' from London, keeping the Great Eastern Railway on its toes. Barges called 'stackies' were piled high with straw with which to feed London's army of 100,000 horses; horse manure for market gardens came back by return. Coal arrived in lighters from large Tyneside colliers anchored downriver, and Hythe Quay any evening might see a Geordie exercising his whippet prior to a pint in the Neptune Inn.

Just up Hythe Hill was Colchester's largest factory, Paxman's, employing 850 men. Their steam engines, boilers and compressors were sold all over the world. From its murky foundry where molten iron ran into moulds, to the fitting shop where engines were assembled, manual skill, born of a lifetime's practice, ruled the day. Work began at 6.30 am and continued to 6 pm. Everyone worked Saturday, with overtime to all hours if an order was urgent. Also at the Hythe the Colchester Lathe Company made lathes, Brackett's made pumps and

One bay of Paxman's large machine shop.

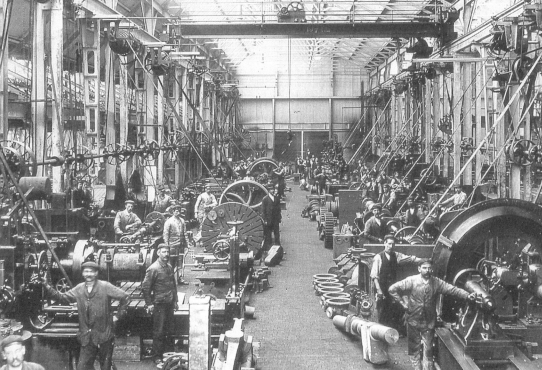

Wood's made electrical fans, while in Culver Street Mumford's employed 400 men building marine engines and pumps. At St Botolph's Corner the Britannia Company, which made lathes and engines, shocked the town by putting 300 men out of work in January 1914. Thus almost 2,000 men worked in engineering, compared to 1,500 in the building trades and under 1,000 in printing.

Transport – trains, trams, horse-drawn wagons – also employed 1,500 men. In 1914 the first wheezing motor buses were rolling into High Street. As the number of cars grew, the number of horse cabs declined, though most goods were still carried by horse and cart. In 1914 urban Colchester was still small by modern standards. Farms and market gardens within the borough employed 800 men. Colchester was a market town and Saturday was market day. Farmers rode in by pony and trap; carriers' carts collected goods for villagers, leaving their horses for the day at one of several inns which had stables. In the morning, livestock was sold at the cattle market in Middleborough; in the afternoon farmers assembled in the Corn Exchange, now the sixth largest in Britain, to buy grain. For shoppers Saturday was the day to come to town.

Farmers assessing sheep in Colchester's livestock market.

Gordon Highlanders leaving from St Botolph's station. Far left on the horizon is Hollington's Clothing Factory.

Last but not least, Colchester was a major garrison town, headquarters of the Eastern Military District. The army occupied a large and growing swathe of land to the south of the town, extending well into the country. The garrison was yet another self-contained world, home in peacetime to a fluctuating 4,000 or so troops in a Colchester population of 43,000. With specialist artillery and cavalry barracks, married quarters, a military hospital, gymnasium, riding school and sports fields, set round the tree-lined Abbey Field, it was a world whose public spaces were open to Colchester's citizens. Regiments came and went and, since these were now regionally recruited, commanding officers made serious efforts to engage with the civilian population.

Troops arriving by rail with their kit and sometimes their horses, led by a regimental band, were, like the coming and going of barges at the Hythe, worth going to see, and once they were in barracks the local press was quick to include news of their activities. Indeed, a column of Garrison News was as regular as Farming Notes in the local papers. Every Sunday morning Colchester turned out to see the men in their kaleidoscope of colourful uniforms: crimson, blue, green, yellow, attending church parade in the historic Garrison Church. Afterwards regimental bands entertained the public as they strolled freely round the Parade Ground.

Army on Parade

Reginald Sillitoe, born 1897

Just before the First World War - now I'm going to tell you the truth. With all the pageantry that London puts on, such as the Lord Mayor's Show... I don't think I've ever in my life seen a more massive show than Colchester used to turn out on a Sunday Morning Church Parade... In those days the public were allowed in the Camp. I've seen as many as eight to 10,000 men on that square opposite the Camp Church... and I've seen eight or nine bands march away to their barracks that surround it – Sobraon, Meeanee, Cavalry Barracks, Artillery, Hydrabad, Googerat... and as they went away, according to as the wind was a-blowing, you would hear Colonel Bogie and 'Goodbye Dolly I must leave you' wafting in the air... Of course the favourite, I think, went to the cavalry... going up that wonderful ride, called in those days the Cavalry Road [now Circular Road] *and, course, that wasn't a McAdam-type road... it was made of a kind of granite flint and on a hot summer's day it was almost like chalk when the wind blew. But to see a regiment of cavalry, practically 1,000 men, with their busbies, their scarlet trousers, the gold braid on their dark blue tunics, and jack boots, and the jingle of the spurs, and the lovely brass band – it's very difficult to narrate. And all for nothing! They was my idols you know. Glittering swords; and as they come into the gates the order would go out 'shun' and the guards would 'eyes right'. And afterwards they would come out and play on the square from 12.30 to 1 o'clock.*

Though soldiers were better fed and paid than ever before, a particular problem attended marriage. The army had long considered its ranks were for young single men, with only senior NCOs being married. Any soldier wishing to wed needed the consent of his commanding officer with just 6 per cent of those in the ranks being the approved maximum. Such couples were termed 'on the strength'. Unsanctioned marriages, termed 'off the strength', were not recognised by the army. They could not live in married quarters, enjoy free accommodation, have any ration

Hussars emerging from a garrison church parade.

Watching army band play after formal church parade was a regular Colchester entertainment.

allowance, pension, medical or educational services. They were, in effect, flung into poverty when a regiment was posted abroad.

Approval to marry was only given after seven years' service, but the new short service enlistments were for six years, increasing the number of off-the-strength wives in the town. During the Boer War, still fresh in the minds of Colchester people, the mayor had raised over £700 (£500,000 in economic value now) for the off-the-strength wives when their husbands were shipped to South Africa. A large and well-provided Soldiers Home in St Botolph's Street and an active branch of the Soldiers & Sailors Families Association which operated under the local Red Cross, gave ongoing support too.

Nor were garrison wives the only issue to worry Colchester's charitable classes. Colchester was a godly town and church and chapel attendance was high. Prostitution had long been a concern and venereal disease was quite widespread: as late as 1900 23 per cent of garrison soldiers were infected. Until 1889 the town had had a specialist Lock

'Last orders': a postcard comment on Colchester's rowdy Saturday nights.

Hospital, placed in garrison towns for young women with sexually transmitted diseases. Seedy public houses were notorious for their accompanying vice, and drunkenness was also a problem. The brewery lobby in Colchester was very vocal, but so was the growing Temperance Movement. Boosted by the presence of so many single young men, Colchester in 1914 had one pub for every 220 residents. Drinking and fighting on Saturday nights was such that the military police kept a constant presence in central Colchester.

In May 1894 history had been made when Gunner Philpotts of the Royal Artillery was found face down and drunk in the urinal of the Cross Keys pub. When he became violent four military pickets carried him away by the so-called 'frog march', face down with his arms and legs extended. Reaching the guardhouse they realised that Philpotts looked very ill. Taken by stretcher to the civilian hospital, he promptly died. Following the inquest, frog marching was abolished by the army and replaced by 'escort under armpits', though the term 'frog marching' has survived till this day. Meanwhile improved canteen and social conditions within the garrison did much to reduce heavy drinking in the ranks and the presence of soldiers in large numbers in Colchester pubs.

Colchester was also home to a large and growing number of retired soldiers, some still on the reserves, settled here because it was a soldier town. This was true of all ranks, and the Lexden Road area, where the army owned properties, housed both serving and retired officers. Ex-soldiers from the ranks took on new occupations, often involving uniforms. They worked in the Post Office and boosted the ranks of the Borough Police Force. They secured jobs as male nurses at the new Severalls Psychiatric Hospital. The Great Eastern Railway employed about 1,000 over its extensive mileage. There was an army Oddfellows' Lodge; they attended Conservative Party smoking concerts. A range of regional accents enriched Colchester neighbourhoods and school playgrounds echoed to Hindi or Urdu oaths picked up by listening to granddad, who served in India.

One more positive consequence of the garrison was the presence in Colchester of a flourishing Territorial Force, amalgamated in 1908 from the existing Militia, Yeomanry and Volunteers. In 1912, when established as the National Reserve, Colchester's contingent numbered 814. They were all part-time soldiers, technically there for local

Group of Volunteers at summer camp, before they were merged into the Territorials

defence. Historically the Militia were rural labourers led by gentry, reinforced by retired and acting soldiers. Their annual camps were held in Colchester. The Yeomanry, a mounted force, were of a higher social class, recruiting among the landed gentry and their tenants. Based in Colchester, the Essex Yeomanry trained on the garrison's Abbey Field, in the Corn Exchange and in the Volunteers' Drill Hall. In 1914 they numbered almost 500.

The Colchester Volunteers were regarded as mere 'Saturday Night Soldiers', but they had an important presence, not least from a social calendar based round their large Drill Hall and rifle range built by Major Howard, a local solicitor and their commanding officer for many years. One of the largest public halls in the town, the Drill Hall housed popular entertainments and political events, often on behalf of the Conservative Party. Many local employers encouraged their men to join the Volunteers who in 1914 formed by far the largest element in the Territorials whose total Colchester numbers ran to about 500, to which can be added 100 or so army reservists.

The military thus permeated and informed many aspects of Colchester's life. Its presence considerably benefitted the local economy, not just from the purchasing power of soldiers, but from contracts for building works, fodder, beer and provisions. The Army bolstered the income of the borough's electricity and water supply and enhanced a range of ceremonial events: the tattoos in Castle Park, the annual town and army St George's Day Parade and the troops in ceremonial uniforms to line the streets for the annual Oyster Feast and other major civic events. Here and at dinners of all kinds the armed forces were regularly toasted. Army sportsmen enhanced the skills level of local football teams and army bands filled the bandstand in Castle Park every summer.

Because it was close to the continent, elaborate war games took place in the district; the Garrison Commander was a major military figure, and the town felt reflected glory from the occasional royal visit. Crowds gathered to see soldiers off at times of war and church bells

Troops clogging Head Street during military manoeuvres.

were rung to celebrate victories. Colchester's MP until 1910 was Sir Weetman Pearson, one of the most prominent Liberal Imperialists in the House. All this helped frame Colchester's mind-set. Edwardian Imperialism had been vividly evident after the Relief of Mafeking during the Boer War; Colchester had a day's holiday and put on a carnival procession. In 1914 the army in Colchester was thus ever-present, and soldiers were by far the largest employed group in the town. Little did they realise that well before Christmas their number would be massively increased.

CHAPTER 2

August 1914

It was proving to be a hot summer. Essex was on holiday. Flower shows were in full swing and the harvest was early. Colchester's Boy Scouts were away at camp and Colchester's first Essex Cricket Week had been crowned with a win by Essex over Worcestershire in Castle Park. Bank Holiday Monday, 3 August, saw the traditional Dabchicks' sailing race at West Mersea and almost 40,000 'excursionists' went to Clacton, mostly by train, some by coastal steamer, others by road on newly acquired motorbikes. Though nearby at Great Clacton, 1,000 Essex Territorial soldiers were holding their summer camp, war did not appear to be on many people's mind. But it was.

Colchester scouts at camp. Sitting centre is their founder, Geoffrey Elwes.

A Bank Holiday paddle steamer arriving at Clacton pier.

In a garrison town like Colchester news spread fast. On 29 July, the weekly garden party at the Officers' Club was in full swing with tea, tennis and chatter, when sharp ears heard a bugle sounding the 'alarm', followed by 'assembly' and 'mobilisation'. As Head of Eastern Command Colchester was the front of the front line. Hurriedly the officers downed their tea, bade farewell to their guests and within an hour were heading for the coast. Their men meanwhile were traced in cinemas and pubs and left by train very early the next day. They would become the 'Old Contemptibles' so called because of the Kaiser's foolish jibe that the British Expeditionary Force was 'a contemptible little army'.

News also filtered through that orders had been sent to the Essex Territorials at Clacton. Within hours the latest arrivals struck camp, while the Essex Yeomanry, summoned from their civilian tasks, were directed to set up camp on Braiswick Golf Course. On the cliffs at Clacton-on-Sea the old Napoleonic Martello Tower became the new base of the Royal Flying Corps, manned from 3 August by three seaplanes. The district was clearly going onto a war footing. Aeroplanes were still so rare a sight that when one had flown over Colchester two weeks before, crowds had run into the street to watch it. For some it was the first plane they had ever seen.

And Colcestrians who read their local paper were aware of the crisis triggered by the assassination in June of Archduke Franz Ferdinand, heir to the Austrian throne. On 28 July Austria had declared war on Serbia, alleged paymaster of his assassin Gavrilo Princep. Both sides appealed to their allies. Russia backed Serbia (then spelt Servia), Austria called in Germany, who knew Russia had a defensive alliance with France. Fearing an attack from both sides, Germany planned to invade France via Belgium before Russia could mobilise. They therefore declared war on both Russia and France. Germany's demand to march through Belgium, in effect to invade Belgium, brought Britain into the war on 4 August. All this took just seven days.

In 1914 Colchester had two main local papers, one Liberal, one Conservative, both broadsheets and eight pages long. They were soon in great demand. The *Essex County Standard* was published on 8 August. Its owner, Gurney Benham, was a leading political figure in the town. Its leader column declared:

ESSEX COUNTY STANDARD

SATURDAY, AUGUST 8, 1914.

THE GREAT WAR

THE long foretold European War has at last become a terrible reality, and there can be no question that in the history of the future Germany, whatever excuses she may now make, will be universally credited with the awful responsibility of having initiated the terrible conflagration. The original spark of the Servian trouble has been taken advantage of by Germany to commence a savage conflict for which the ostensible pretext is plainly no real cause. Mad ambitions as to her "destiny" and wild notions as to the overwhelming power of her armaments with a greed for the supremacy of the civilised world, are the real sources and springs of all this terrible catastrophe. She is the NAPOLEON of the 20th Century, heedless of all things but those wild ambitions of her own, regardless of the sufferings of millions of people, of

The Essex County Standard *announces The GREAT WAR, caused by Germany ambition.*

The retrospect of the last seven days is like an incredible and detestable dream. The worst pessimist could hardly have imagined a week crowded with such a succession of bad news. Never were Colchester people so obsessed with one subject as on Wednesday, when they awoke to find that England was at war with Germany. Yet there was no hysterical excitement. The crowds that lined the streets in the evening waited calmly and patiently for news.

In the absence of radio, televison and the internet that news came from the High Street office of the *Essex County Standard*, and the Head Street office of the *Essex County Telegraph*, who both placed bulletins in their windows, and from the columns of the *Colchester Gazette* which came out on Wednesdays. Ahead of the history books the leader column ran the caption THE GREAT WAR, and left little doubt as to who was to blame. Here, if any were needed, is evidence of a mood and attitude in Colchester. It was a mood defined by a Colchester middle class schooled to lead from the front, epitomised in the editorial of the Colchester Royal Grammar School's magazine:

> *When the summer term closed... with a vision of a happy and peaceful holiday... not even the most daring of prophets would have ventured to foretell that in the space of a fortnight the whole of Europe would have flashed into a blaze...*
>
> *It has been brought about by no mere assassination, no impossible ultimatum... It is part of the eternal strife between Right and Might, Justice and Privilege, Liberty and Tyranny... Christianity and Paganism that reappears in all ages... There can be but one end. The Prussian menace must go... And this nation... will see to it that 'peace and happiness, truth and justice, religion and piety, shall be established among us for all generations.'*

It was a mood firmly supported by the Churches, particularly the Church of England, itself a major pillar of the Establishment both nationally and locally. On the first Sunday of the war, 9 August, all Colchester churches had focused on the war, still somewhat bewildered by events. By Sunday 21 August, which was declared a National Day of Prayer, an official line had become more clear. All Colchester churches, Anglican, Nonconformist and Catholic, participated, with a grand civic service at St Peter's in the afternoon at which the Bishop of Colchester preached, his sermon reproduced in full in the *Essex County Standard*. Simultaneously a 'service for all' took place at St Nicholas which was addressed by the Bishop of Chelmsford. Both men argued that this was a righteous war, taken up in defence of Belgium against German barbarity; that it was a patriotic war to uphold the moral mission for which Britain and the British Empire stood. Christian manliness was called for as men were urged to volunteer. These were themes that would echo in both press and public meetings throughout the early months of the conflict.

Meanwhile, in the street and in the workplace a mood of crisis excitement engulfed Colchester. Spy scares filled the first few days of the war. Two alleged spies were arrested near the barracks; another was followed by a crowd all the way to the police station. Local boy scouts, already acting as messengers for the military, were organised into night-time patrols, guarding bridges and telephone wires from Marks Tey to Stratford St Mary against sabotage by spies. Wallace Cole, the District Scoutmaster, was freed from all duties by his employers, so that he could supervise these vital activities. Quite who all these spies were was less clear, but anyone who had seen a German – tourist, visitor or UK resident – in the previous few years searched their mind for any hint of suspicious behaviour. Unsurprisingly, some found it.

Germans were studious observers of historic and cultural sites. They took photographs. With Colchester so close to the East Coast where an invasion force might land, such cultural tourists could be recast as spies. Gurney Benham, an eager historian, filled his own column in the *Essex County Standard* with tales of how Colchester had faced possible

Built to repel Napoleonic invaders 100 year before, Clacton's main Martello Tower now became a base for Britain's fledgling air force. (Norman Jacobs collection)

invasion by Napoleon 100 years before. At Clacton a German with a camera inspecting the old Martello Tower two days before war began was arrested. He turned out to be 16-years-old and interested in history. An innocent Norwegian watching troops and equipment being loaded at St Botolph's station on the second day of war was arrested by military police and later released, but the story still made the local paper.

Letters appeared in the press: two German 'officers' seen the previous summer cycling round the Tendring Hundred taking photographs and *doing measurements*, had clearly been spies. Across South Essex, from West Ham to Southend, German shopkeepers were targeted, even attacked when, in December, East Coast towns were shelled and civilians killed. It happened again in 1915 when the *Lusitania* was sunk. No German was attacked in Colchester, but two local shopkeepers with foreign names felt the need to write to the papers saying they were not German. The Rev George Behr, Rector of St Stephen's Church and son of a naturalised German, lamented in his parish magazine that

> *I have been put to some inconvenience, and not only I, but my mother and sister also, because some 'busy people' have set going a story that we are German and not only that, but German spies... even our two collie dogs have been trained for no good purpose...*

Fortunately, there were other respected ethnic Germans in the district, several of whom would fight on the British side, even a few veterans of the popular German Legion, who had settled in Colchester after the Crimean War, and whose children lived here still. Such facts prevented unpleasant incidents. So did a letter to the local press from the much-respected mayor, Wilson Marriage, recalling Colchester's long acceptance of refugees and foreigners, who should not be demonised merely because of their place of birth. There was, nevertheless, a government order to arrest all Germans of military age. Emma, the daughter of Councillor Jarmin who would become mayor in 1917, was engaged to an Austrian architect, Tommy Rehberger. In 1990, aged 102, she recalled:

There were rumours of war… My Father said, 'If you don't want to be a prisoner of war, you'd better get married and be a prisoner of war in England'. It was a good thing in the long run. We got a house and had our first little girl.

Initially interned on the Isle of Man, Rehberger was released to work on a farm in Yorkshire. On the other hand, while Hythe residents complained about the smell from Wombach's factory, no one seemed worried that its owners were of German extraction.

With war declared, large numbers of Colchester men who were Reservists or Territorials left to join their colours. For the Colchester Territorials, now the Fifth Battalion of the Essex Regiment, this initially meant coastal duty at Dovercourt, but within days they were drafted to Harwich for immediate embarkation. They included, for example, 141 men from Paxman's and sixty from Mumford's, the town's two largest engineering firms, and one third of the Colchester Lathe Company's eighty-man workforce, all skilled men. Soon there would be 113 more skilled men from Spottiswoode's, the printers. All these volunteers were guaranteed their jobs back when the war was over, but the loss of their skills would soon be an issue. Bandsman Victor Sawyer of the Rifle Brigade recalled:

'We found Meeanee Barracks full of reservists – many still in civilian dress – and more were flocking in by almost every train. Fitting them out with uniform, boots and equipment was proceeding rapidly, but in some cases was no easy job, as quite a few men had lost that soldierly figure they had taken with them into civilian life and… were now portly.'

From Day One the gates of the garrison were shut – something unknown before – and soldiers with fixed bayonets stood guard. Within two weeks four regiments stationed in the garrison, the First Battalion Somerset Light Infantry, the First East Lancashires, the First Hampshires and the First Rifle Brigade, perhaps 3,000 men all told, left for Harrow, arriving in France within days. Two days later the 20th Hussars, a cavalry regiment, left too, coaxing their horses with some difficulty into the specialist railway trucks.

The logistical demands of these troop movements led the military

These once open gates of Meeanee Barracks would now be closed to the public.

to take control of St Botolph's railway station (today Colchester Town), closing it to civilian use. Motorcars, coal waggons, corporation carts, Co-Op vans and motor buses were requisitioned to carry stores to the station. One officer, taking a squad of soldiers to Chelmsford, stopped a tram in Head Street and ordered it to reverse and take them to North Station. Moving men and materials went on all night, assisted by the erection of arc lights over the St Botolph's goods yard. Late-night bystanders watched with fascination.

The first impact on the town of the declaration of war was a rush to hoard provisions. From Day Two there was an armed guard on the main Post Office in Head Street, on Jumbo the water tower and on Marriage's East Mills, sources of those vital products: communications, water and bread. Britain now only grew 20 per cent of its wheat. Though wheat from America might be safely expected, Russia's Ukraine, another major source, might be cut off by war. Despite the assurance of its manager that, with a good harvest coming in, at least three month's supply of wheat existed, there was a run on East Mill's flour which rose by eight shillings a sack. Some 50 per cent of Britain's meat and 65 per cent of its dairy products were imported too. Food shops underwent a minor siege. Prices rose. The Colchester & East Essex Co-Op announced that it would restrict customers to their normal orders to prevent a run on food. Not all food shops felt the same, as this letter to a local newspaper made clear,

> *Sir,*
> *Through the medium of your columns I would like to place on record my profound disgust at the closing of no less than eight prominent provision establishments in the town during the whole of yesterday to execute huge orders received from persons who, having the means at their disposal, were enabled to lay in a vast stock of food to the detriment of the poorer classes, whose consideration should be no less than those who can afford to have 'their bread buttered on both sides'.*

A second consequence of war was the feared loss of work at Colchester's factories. The clothing firms were soon only working half-time as many export orders were cancelled, but Colchester's MP, Worthington Evans, pulled strings to get some major orders for

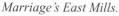

Marriage's East Mills.

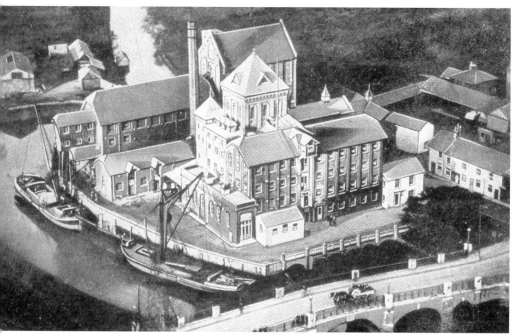

uniforms placed in Colchester. Wilkin's jam factory at Tiptree imported much of its sugar from Germany and a consignment due for shipment at Hamburg was stopped by the German government. On 4 August the chairman, Charles Wilkin, rushed to London to sell some securities and buy sugar for cash, but the Stock Exchange had been closed so he could not sell his securities, while the giant Tate & Lyle refinery on the Thames was expecting to be taken over by the government any day. However on 16 August at a meeting in Whitehall, Wilkin and the other major jam manufacturers of Britain brokered a deal whereby they would supply all the jam needs of the nation in return for continued autonomy. Despite this reprieve the Tiptree factory was at a standstill by December.

On the declaration of war James Paxman, owner of Colchester's largest business, had telegrammed the Prime Minister, Herbert Asquith:

> *Humbly implore you to...call up one or even two million men to arms..... My firm Davey, Paxman & Company willing to put aside all orders and devote itself entirely to government service....*

Work inside the Tiptree Jam Factory (The John Wilkin Collection).

He also cabled the First Lord of the Admiralty, Winston Churchill. Did Churchill know that German submarines could be detected by electricity? There is no evidence that either men replied, but soon Paxman's became one of three British firms identified for 'secret' Admiralty work, designing and building the so-called 'otters', code name for booms floating either side of a ship, towing a 200-foot wire which severed German mines from their sinkers, a process that was to prove 100 per cent successful throughout the war. It was the start of a busy time for Paxman's, and that growth in central government which would change Britain for ever. Already Paxman's had been working all night to provide a steam engine and generator needed in Egypt to complete a government chain of radio communications. This was going to be a world war.

Meanwhile Colchester preferred, as had been its habit, to run itself. This however was not to be, as central government became dramatically interventionist. As the *Standard* reported, when the town's Provisional Relief Committee had met for the first time on 7 August, 'the mayor had been waited on by a government official who had pointed out the desirability of not taking independent action' – the government intended to control things themselves. The following day they passed the Defence of the Realm Act, hereafter called by its popular acronym, DORA. Initially designed to cope with potential invasion and give central government wide-ranging powers to wage war, its most immediate consequence was government requisitioning of factories, land, railways, harbours, vehicles, horses – the list is considerable; its most problematic consequence would be its expanding powers of censorship. By October the mayor was observing that Colchester was now 'virtually under martial law'.

The Local Government Board duly proposed a Local Relief Committee. Chaired by the mayor, Wilson Marriage, a pacifist Quaker, it included the deputy mayor, William Coats Hutton, his formidable wife, Ethel, Major-General Hunter-Wilson, the Garrison Commander, Colonel Stockwell, the Chief Constable (Colchester had its own fifty-seven-

William Coats Hutton.

strong police force), Percy Sanders who ran Paxman's engineering
works, Alderman Gurney Benham, newspaper owner, and a handful of
clergy and leading councillors. It took for its headquarters the Albert
School in High Street, formerly the Albert School of Science & Art,
now tentatively seeking to become an art gallery following the opening
of the new art school and technical school on North Hill (today the

The Albert School of Art in its education days.

Sixth Form College). In a crucial change of direction the Albert School now became the focus for a host of war-related initiatives outside the remit of the town council, physically separated from that bastion of civic power, the town hall.

The Relief Committee first initiated a public subscription to the Prince of Wales Relief Fund, set up to aid those penalised by the outbreak of war. In the best Victorian tradition it was truly public. Over the next three weeks the names and amounts given were printed in the local press of 372 donors, mostly individuals, plus a few by local businesses, of sums ranging from over £1,000 to five shillings. This practice underlines the extent to which Colchester was still a face-to-face society where, within the middle classes, almost everyone knew, or knew of, everyone else. With this went a fairly shrewd knowledge of their wealth, if not their personal lives. It was therefore 'noticed' if your name was missing from the list, or if your subscription was far below your cash potential. After this 'public' subscriptions came workplace, church and street collections of modest sums from ordinary people who, unlike the great and the good, remained anonymous.

Part of the public subscription to the Prince of Wales Fund.

The Relief Committee now reviewed the problems facing the families of departing servicemen and those economically disadvantaged by the outbreak of war: who had lost their job, for example. The town was divided into ten districts, each with its own committee. Their task was made easier by the government's decision to make regular payments to wives and families of regular soldiers 'off the strength', payments made via the local branch of the Soldiers and Sailors Families Association. Colchester again was well placed with two of the County Representatives, Lady Digby and Mrs Sanders (mother of Percy Sanders), resident in the district. Details of how this functioned are covered in Chapter 5. Colchester's town council now proposed to alleviate any unemployment caused by the disruptions of war with thirteen suggested road-widening schemes. In fact this did not prove necessary: compared with most other towns Colchester had few unemployed.

Alderman Gurney Benham, newspaper owner.

There was also a swift move to stabilise food sales and prices. This was achieved by good example and corporate pressure. A block advertisement appeared in all three newspapers signed by the President of the Colchester Chamber of Commerce, Wilson Marriage, and its chairman, Gurney Benham, to say that local shopkeepers would 'keep to normal prices to the extreme limit possible', an inelegant phrase clearly written by a lawyer, and not by Gurney Benham himself. In return, the bulletin continued, Colchester shoppers should regard it as 'their patriotic duty' to shop locally to enable their shopkeepers to fulfil this promise. Matters were helped by a report in the same paper that Canada, which was sending both troops and arms, had also promised to set aside 90 million tons of flour for Britain.

On the instruction of the local justices of the peace, and without consulting the licensees' own association, Colchester pubs were all shut every night at 9 pm 'to prevent soldiers rendering themselves unfit for training'. Under the terms of DORA, Colchester's Chief Constable,

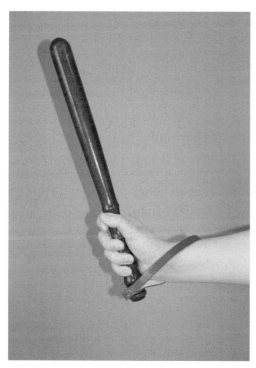

The truncheon and badge of a Colchester Special Constable in the Great War.
(Colchester & Ipswich Museum Service)

Colonel Stockwell swore in seventy-eight special constables, beginning with Special No 1, Wilson Marriage, issuing them with armbands, whistles and truncheons. Stockwell soon wanted yet more 'Specials' and before the year ended there were nearly ninety. Law and order was an important consideration, for Colchester was fast filling up with young men.

The legendary 'rush to the colours' had begun, an extraordinary period marked by a mood of heightened enthusiasm, driven by genuine patriotism, the response of an island nation that had not seen real war for fifty years. Crowds attended troop departures at train stations and sang the National Anthem, while otherwise restrained young women dashed into the road to kiss soldiers as they marched off to war. They called it 'khaki fever'. With regulars and volunteers marching everywhere in Colchester, the sense of excitement was palpable. The local press, already becoming the government's cheerleader, focused particularly on the drama of men enlisting in their hundreds, responding spontaneously to fight for their country.

Colchester was one of three main recruiting centres in Essex. Not only Colchester's young men but those from a wide rural area, embracing the entire Tendring Hundred, descended on the town. Colchester's small recruiting office on Port Lane was soon overwhelmed. From 31 August, the Borough transferred recruitment to the Albert School in High Street. The new office was immediately very busy. Worthington Evans, the town's MP, came to be seen and to give his support. Round the corner on North Hill the vicar of St Peter's Church (the civic church), Rev Triffit Ward, opened his parish room for new recruits to use as a waiting room. The hall became so crowded that he invited them into his garden too. Light refreshments were provided for the many 'sturdy young men from the countryside' arriving by car – itself a source of great excitement for them. But, as the press explained, there was often no other way to get them to Colchester for their medical inspection and their formal attestation to serve King and Country.

St Peter's Church, at the top of North Hill, has been the civic church of Colchester for over 200 years.

Villages feeding into this process must have witnessed scenes similar to those over three days at St Osyth's:

Their send off when leaving on Monday was an enthusiastic one, but that word is quite inadequate to express the tremendous feeling shown when on Wednesday at 1.30 the eleven men who had been passed left... in motors kindly lent by Mrs Cowley and Mr Vincent. Apparently nearly all the inhabitants of the village were present and there was an immense amount of cheering as the motors started on their journey to Colchester.

Such send offs were often preceded by meetings in village halls, the platform crammed with JPs, gentry and the occasional MP. After a few words from the VIP chairman, a hymn was frequently sung, followed by a stirring recruitment speech and often the National Anthem.

After one week Colchester's more central recruitment office could barely cope. A newspaper reported that '500 have volunteered in Colchester so far, 200 from the borough'. A second Colchester paper provides much the same picture, giving the week's total as 689 with 50 still waiting at closing time on Friday. Given that late August and early September was the peak recruitment period for Colchester, with more volunteers in the first few days of September than all of October, these are not outstanding numbers, but we need to remember that many Colchester Reservists and Territorials were already in uniform and Colchester was already reading about how they were getting on.

From the outset Colchester and its villages turned to the local press as well as the national dailies for news of the war. This was in part because of the regional regimental system. The *Standard*, the *Telegraph* and the *Gazette* followed the fortunes of Essex servicemen, providing, alongside local news, the unfolding story of what would become the Western Front, where trenches were dug, and armies would spend four years fighting a war of attrition. A 'diary' listing the chief events of the war was regularly published, expanded week by week. A large map of Western Europe, showing the chief theatres of war, appeared in every edition. Contrary to many claims that civilians were kept in the dark about the nature of the war, during this first autumn, indeed the first year, the realities of war and the cost in lives could plainly be read in the local paper.

Obituaries soon appeared and graphic accounts of combat written

GERMANS MAKE NO PROGRESS.

THE RUSSIAN ADVANCE.

CRUISER "HERMES" TORPEDOED NEAR DOVER.

FLEET SURGEON MOWAT, OF DOVERCOURT, AMONG THE RESCUED.

MYSTERY OF TURKISH WAR OPERATIONS.

WOUNDED BELGIAN SOLDIERS AT THORPE LE SOKEN.

N.B.—All items marked † are unofficial and must be accepted with reserve.

THE BATTLES IN BELGIUM AND FRANCE.

TURKEY DIVIDED AGAINST ITSELF.

RUSSIAN ADVANCE CONTINUES †

NORTH SEA DECLARED "A MILITARY AREA."

NAVAL ENGAGEMENT OFF NORFOLK COAST

CRUISER "HERMES" SUNK IN STRAITS OF DOVER.

LOCAL WAR ITEMS.

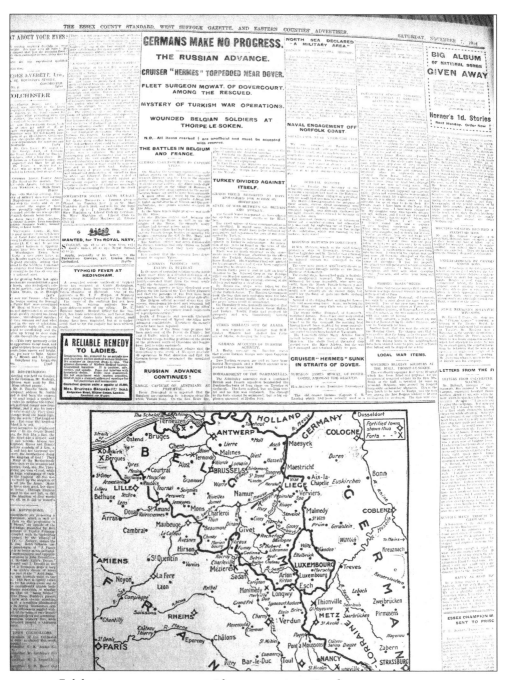

Colchester newspapers gave wide coverage to national war news.

in personal letters were printed by the local press, as well as interviews with wounded soldiers arriving home. Despite a sometimes gung-ho bravado – '*I've lost one leg, but I've still got the other to beat the Germans*' – reality still filtered through. Soon there were the trainloads of wounded arriving at Colchester Station. Then there was word of mouth. The street, the friends and the relatives soon knew if a mother received a letter recording the death of her son. And from the outset the town swarmed with rumours, which have a familiar ring. Russian cavalry were seen 'with snow on their boots' passing through Colchester by train, 'their black horses clearly visible'. Another myth of the Great War, 'The Angel of Mons', in which celestial beings had protected the British army at the Battle of Mons, received one of its earliest airing in the St Mary's Parish Magazine.

As a responsible newspaper editor, Gurney Benham regularly placed the symbol † against news items not verified by official sources, but, as the war progressed, government sources started to become

Shaming the shirkers – a cartoon from the Essex County Standard.

suspect too, and censorship more marked. All the Colchester newspapers vigorously recruited for Kitchener's Army, initially with advertisements filling an entire page and soon with regular cartoons, supplied from official sources, vilifying the Germans or seeking to shame men into enlisting. But the impact of this may have been short lived. This was a garrison town. The harsher realities of military life and what was actually happening on the Western Front soon reached those citizens who did not read the paper or live anywhere near the middle class strongholds of Lexden Road.

Meanwhile the expansion of the garrison continued. As August progressed some fifteen regular army battalions moved into Colchester, replacing those who were now in France. Within days of Kitchener's famous appeal for 100,000 men, Colchester was also selected to train many of his Volunteers. In late August 2,000 recruits arrived from London, marching up Mersea Road still dressed in their civilian clothes. By 25 September there were over 20,000 troops, regulars and Volunteers, in the town, compared with a peace-time garrison of 4,000. Occasionally over the next three years numbers touched 40,000, matching the civilian population. There had not been so many soldiers in Colchester, declared Gurney Benham, since the time of Boadicea. All these troops put pressure on the district in many, many ways, but they were very good news for Colchester's shopkeepers, and it is the impact of this great invasion on the district to which we must now turn.

Kitchener Volunteers arriving from London, march past the barracks on Mersea Road in their civilian clothes.

CHAPTER 3

The Great Invasion

Throughout the four long years of the war Colchester's vast Abbey Field remained a place to visit for Colchester residents with the time to spare. Here you could see a mustering of soldiers such as the town had not seen before and would never see again. And they were 'good' soldiers, cast in the Boys Own Paper image of cheerful, healthy, smart young men, getting fit and ready to fight for King and Country. It fitted the national outburst of patriotic excitement. And on the Abbey Field no one was getting killed.

This formal photo gives some idea of the size of Abbey Field. The distant horizon is Circular Road South, with the Cavalry and Artillery Barracks. Additional tent accommodation can just be seen there.

Kitchener's Army was the cream of the nation; not your traditional Edwardian squaddies from disadvantaged backgrounds and poor educational attainment, men whose reputation, deserved or exaggerated, led Colchester mothers to warn their daughters to avoid soldiers. Kitchener's 'boys' were citizen soldiers, inspired to serve their country, mostly from 'good homes', often skilled workers, who, as the flood of recruits from Colchester demonstrated, would never consider the Army as a career or want to be called 'Tommy Atkins'. As the government soon discovered the national response to Kitchener's appeal was extraordinary. From half a million, to one million, the volunteer army grew to nearly two and a half million by Christmas 1915. Merely to accommodate, let alone equip, this host presented a national challenge which Colchester, like centres throughout the country, had to face.

Kitchener Volunteers, still in civilian clothes, introduced to the joys of drill at Meeanee Barracks. (Colchester & Ipswich Museum Service).

Initially they were housed in a sea of tents all over the Abbey Field and Reed Hall beyond, all over the Recreation Ground on Old Heath Road; up at a large new camp at Mile End; out at Wivenhoe Park, the estate of the Gooch family (now the University of Essex) where deer still roamed; in the grounds of Lexden Park, home of the Sanders family; up at the golf course on Bergholt Road; and across the 'Siberian

Fully kitted out, these Kitchener Volunteers and their benign Quartermaster Sergeant were attached to the Catering Unit.

Wastes' of Middlewick, the Army's extensive firing ranges, where Colchester's adventurous kids regularly trespassed in search of excitement and the scrap value of spent bullet cases. Where you could pitch no tents, empty buildings would do instead. Down in Wivenhoe over a hundred were housed on Ballast Quay, in the Forester's Hall, the Masonic Hall and an assortment of empty yacht sheds. Some 5,000 officers and men of the Norfolk and Suffolk Territorials were settled in the grounds of Severalls Psychiatric Hospital, which had only opened the previous year, spawning another tent city, overflowing into several assorted outbuildings.

Challenges inevitably arose at all these venues when weather broke in mid-September. Tents, and the beds inside them, on Abbey Field and at the Mile End Camp were soaked by surface drainage, the messing marquee at Reed Hall blew down, and the field (still there) behind Lexden Park was flooded, its saturated Royal Army Medical Corps (RAMC) volunteers welcomed into neighbouring houses. The trainees all took it in good part, according to the papers. If so, it was a mild

A hot selling postcard while the Suffolks were training in Colchester.

Don't be Alarmed, the Suffolks are on guard at Colchester.

introduction to what was to come on Flanders Field. In October 180 wooden huts each housing up to twenty-two men were erected at Reed Hall. A further 180 went up at Middlewick. This was the start of a veritable hut city at Reed Hall which expanded as autumn turned to winter and living in tents became seriously unpleasant. Another hut city arose at Mile End. Over time not all the huts proved watertight, however.

Simultaneously, billeting with local families was extended, with recruits sharing the one spare bedroom or sleeping on the floor of the sitting room. Billeting was not strictly optional; it was required by the Army Act, but it was achieved by negotiation. It was also remarkably successful, thanks to the goodwill of Colchester householders, the good behaviour of the Volunteer soldiers and a strict tariff of payments set out in the Army Act. For many a poor household or wife with a large

Kitchener boys, happy in their Reed Hall hut, dress up for a joke photo after their Sunday football. (Jess Jephcott collection).

family and a husband at war, it was a vital extra source of income, however modest it might appear to us.

Householders were paid 6d (later 9d) per soldier per night for accommodation plus 'salt, vinegar and the use of the kitchen fire (i.e. the range)' to cook their own food. With this the householder also had to meet the consequent laundry costs. Thereafter the householder was paid 7½d for a breakfast, 1s 7½d for a dinner, 4½d a supper. One enterprising Colchester coal merchant advertised in the paper his 'dreadnought' coals so combustible that a kitchen range could easily handle the extra cooking required. Without breakfast this made a day rate of 2s 6d, though in practice some regiments paid more. An Army Order made clear what meals should be provided for this pay. They are an interesting comment on late Edwardian diets:

Breakfast: five ounces of bread, one pint of tea with milk and sugar, four ounces of bacon.
Hot Dinner (i.e. lunch): twelve ounces of meat (previous to being dressed), four ounces of bread, eight ounces of potatoes or other vegetable.

Supper: five ounces of bread, one pint of cocoa with milk and sugar, two ounces of cheese.

Far more was paid if you accommodated an officer – assuming you had accommodation suitable for an officer. For this, payment was three shillings a night. Finally, the many small stables in Colchester, a town still dependent on horses, might be used by the military too. For stabling, the army paid 9d per horse per day, but if 10lbs of oats, 12lbs of hay and 8lbs of straw were also supplied it was 2s 7½d per horse per day – slightly more than a soldier.

There were thus a variety of domestic billeting experiences with anything from three to no shared meals a day. Nevertheless, many households, though not required to do so, made their 'boys' part of the family. The local press noted that less use was being made of the various clubs set up for soldiers now that they were 'safely housed for winter quarters on the citizens of Colchester'. Oral history makes clear (see Ella Caney) that they might continue to write to the family when

'Part of the family': soldiers billeted in Wivenhoe photographed with their hosts.

drafted overseas, and friendships were formed which could continue for years to come.

The only dispute to come before the local court actually demonstrates the success of the operation. Herbert Russell of Canterbury Road and his wife housed five soldiers in one room. When these left, Mrs Russell scrubbed and fumigated the room before five more replaced them. She was taken so badly ill after doing this that her husband decided to take her to the hospital, a considerable journey across town. Two of the replacement soldiers had meanwhile arrived and left their kit with the Russells. Mr Russell put this in his yard, thinking it might be illegal to lock it in his house, well that's what he claimed. The army now prosecuted him for leaving it there. His potential £5 fine was remitted by the magistrates, who considered the circumstances 'exceptional'. While we might be disinclined to prosecute at all, we might also conclude that if this was the only case the army brought against Colchester billeters, billeting was a great success. For by Christmas 1914 some 1,454 troops were housed in 1,043 civilian billets.

The borough's Inspector of Nuisances, normally occupied with monitoring waste disposal and complaints about Wombachs, now found himself inspecting 1,043 billets, checking cleanliness and monitoring for illness. Like Mrs Russell he found it necessary to fumigate, some soldiers being infected with lice. Arrangements were made to have such bedding treated, along with blankets and paliasses from the expanding hut cities, at the Infectious Diseases Hospital at Mile End.

KITCHENER'S ARMY RECALLED

Jack Ashton, born 1902
My memory most of all is Kitchener's Army coming up Mersea Road. They all had civvy clothes on, you know, just as they'd been called up. And they put them up at Abbey Field under canvas and they fitted those chaps out with blue suits and little hats. And you could have gone up there, and I know people who did go up there, and buy a watch for a bob [1s.] or a good suit for a couple of bob or something like that, because after they got their regimentals they didn't want to be bothered with their

old things; and Butt Road was flooded with them coming into town, and that's when the tradesmen of Colchester did the best trade of their lives.

Sonny Cracknell, born 1906

There were lots and lots of soldiers, and they used to march from the barracks to Clacton every day at 8 o'clock in the morning. So we boys had a glorious excuse for not going to school [on time] *because if we got on the opposite side of the road from Barrack Street School, we couldn't cross the road because we couldn't break the soldiers' ranks! They used all horses then and they used to come down with the 'kitchens' on their backs for cooking, and all the steam a-going up and cooking all the potatoes and what not. And they'd stop after 8 or 9 mile on the side of the road and have their meal, then march to Clacton, and back again at night. And to see these soldiers, some were only about 16,* [having lied about their age] *and their feet were so sore they had their shoes hung on their shoulders and they were walking back just in their socks. And my mother was very kind hearted and used to make mugs of tea and us boys would run alongside – and they always expected it, so the band would strike up just as they got to Hythe Bridge and they would play like anything, and they'd sing, '*... long way to Tipperary*'.*

Ella Caney, born 1897

I remember Kitchener's Army coming into town and they shoved them anywhere they could... Different regiments would come into town and an officer would come round and you might be shopping... So, if you were not at home, that same night they would bring round two or three men or whatever the house could accommodate. They paid you sixpence a night for privates – no laundry or food, just give them decent accommodation... We got some lovely lads. It was dreadful to see them go; and to hear them – we always knew when they were going to be sent to the Front... They were boys who could have come from our own home, good homes, and they would get lonesome and gather in Morant Road at night and sing all the old songs, you know? And there was no rowdiness or anything. Later on [after conscription began] *it was different; you got all the scrapings.... The first boys were the cream of the lot. And they wrote to my sister and myself after they got overseas, but some of them never came back, of course.*

Frank Blandon, born 1905
We had two blokes from the Sussex Regiment in our house. Course, my two brothers were away in the Army, some of the others were married, and there were 4 or 5 of us still at home – kids going to school. And these chaps were a godsend really, 'cos you got paid for having them. On top of that they used to go and draw their rations and they'd scrounge whatever they could for the kids.... tin of jam or extra loaf of bread or a bit of meat, anything they could.

Having somehow accommodated this great army, the Colchester garrison now had problems equipping them. Appeals were made in local papers for underwear and shirts, many men being short of these.

Kitchener probationers on the march wearing their stable caps and 'blues', allegedly surplus post office uniforms.

Cheeky postcards sold in numbers in the winter of 1914-15.

There was even an appeal for boots for recruits 'not able to be supplied by the government'. All over Colchester women and children were knitting socks for soldiers and, as winter came on, scarves and mufflers too. Meanwhile, kitted out in the blue suits and stable caps of probationers, Kitchener's boys poured into town. Though not paid very much, volunteers were happy to sell personal items to finance their short stay. All forms of entertainment benefitted. Visits to the Castle Museum and the cinemas soared. Barbers were kept busy supplying haircuts, and Colchester's trams finally made a profit, charging soldiers in uniform 1d for a journey of any length. In the first year this supplied 57 per cent of the network's annual takings.

One of the first things a new recruit did was send a letter or postcard home. The Post Office in Head Street was besieged by messengers

We are completing our Training at COLCHESTER.

A postcard designed for the Colchester troops in training.

coming to and fro with telegrams and wires; those 'running' for the military were often local boy scouts. With schools now fully functional the mayor solemnly announced that boy scouts acting as army orderlies could be absent from school for a maximum of two weeks. That must have made the job even more attractive. The Post Office felt the extra demand on its services. Postcard sales to army recruits flourished: initially of photographs of local scenes but, before long, of mildly saucy, mass-produced, comic postcards targeting the new recruit market, often overprinted with a reference to the town concerned, in this case Colchester. At Christmas 1914 the Post Office's workload was a record 50 per cent higher than the year before.

Merchants with fixed contracts to supply forage and provisions to the garrison found their orders multiplied, significant laundry contracts were placed in the town, carpenters erected hundreds of army huts and one cycle shop hit the jackpot gaining the contract to service the many bicycles of the Essex Cycle Battalion at the cavalry barracks. Even the black economy benefitted. Albert Cook, brewer of Magdalen Street, was found guilty of selling 570 gallons of beer to three 'cottagers' who then sold it on to the troops. Christmas 1914 was particularly good for the legitimate market too. The wine merchants Lay & Wheeler, who also bottled Guinness, on Christmas Eve had a queue of soldiers stretching from their shop all the way down the High Street and round the corner into Head Street. The downside of this booming trade was a 25 per cent rise in the price of a basket of goods before the war was a year old. This would have long-term consequences.

With the town's population more than 50 per cent larger, the strain on infrastructure was considerable. Roads, still mostly surfaced with ground flints, took a heavy hammering as the army acquired more cars and lorries, carrying goods and equipment either to the garrison or right through the town, since the main road from London to Ipswich and the East Coast ran through central Colchester, via Lexden Road, Head Street, High Street and East Hill. And not just traffic. The constant marching of troops up Shrub End Road, Drury Road and Straight Road,

Recruits on the march in St John's Street are now fully uniformed.

Watering horses and enjoying a smoke in middle class Inglis Road.

Lexden, all still semi-rural, led to significant repair bills. The pre-war plan to cover Head Street and High Street with tarred wooden blocks hit problems: problems of access to mains services, problems of labour and material shortages. In November it was stopped until the spring. The town's sewage works, faced with a 36 per cent increase in the volume of sewage, had to keep pumping both night and day, forcing the borough to both pay overtime and employ more men. Even the weekly removal of refuse from all the new garrison centres came at a cost, which, as a borough service, Colchester absorbed. The Army of course paid for all these services, but paperwork and man-hours increased.

Water supply for the many tent communities was the challenge of the Royal Engineers. It was not just the troops, a single horse needed ten to fourteen gallons of water a day for drinking, grooming and stable maintenance. Down at Wivenhoe the local fire brigade supplied the RAMC on Ballast Quay with 500 gallons of water a day. By 1915 water shortage was becoming a Colchester problem and ancient springs used to wash and service locomotives at North Station were brought back into the town's main supply. Watering of gardens was discouraged and the town council discussed reducing the summer use of water carts to 'lay the dust' on the borough's main roads. By contrast the electricity

Troop movements causing traffic jams at Headgate Corner.

works saw a loss of income as blackout restrictions were slowly enforced.

Up at Severalls Hospital, still struggling from the loss of twenty-one male staff to the Reserves, water shortage and sewage overload spawned sickness. Scarlet fever broke out among the female patients and nurses. Several died. This was followed by influenza which raged throughout the winter. The following winter both flu and typhoid broke out and continued until 1918. It is a credit to army efficiency that more health problems did not afflict the thousands of recruits with their communal lifestyle. A serious outbreak of Spotted Fever (meningococcal meningitis), which travelled across Essex, possibly from military units at Chelmsford, hit the Reed Hall huts, but was soon contained.

With pubs shutting early, how the young recruits might spend their evenings become a matter of civic concern. Initially they walked the streets. In remarkably short time local churches, charities and social groups spawned no fewer than thirty-five clubs and restrooms where troops could drink tea, write letters, play games, or be entertained. One was even set up for the estimated 2,000 wives and children of Kitchener Volunteers who had moved into the town where their husbands were

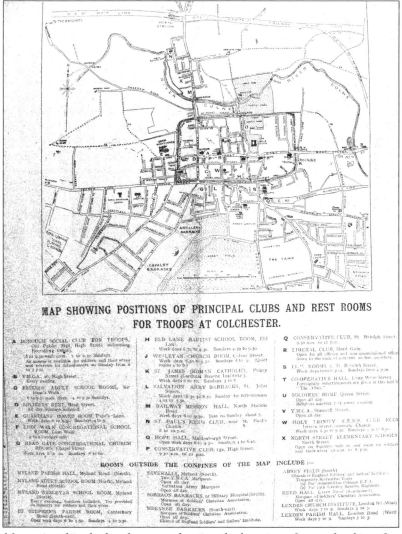

Map printed in the local papers showing the location of some the thirty-five Social Clubs for troops.

training, while another centre taught basic French to help soldiers cope with the locals when they reached France. A street map of Colchester, showing where all these clubs were, was published in every edition of the local papers. Half were in church or chapel premises.

The Nonconformists led the way. The local Quakers, a body noted for their pacifist stance, opened up their premises in Sir Isaac's Walk which for many years had been running a successful programme of adult education. This hall of learning now echoed to troops roaring out *Tipperary* at specially organised entertainments. At the same time the Congregationalists at Headgate Chapel used their Sunday School (today, a restaurant) for a similar purpose. Before long Anglican church halls were following suit, while the Soldiers Home in Queen Street found itself busier than ever before.

Colchester's large Co-op Hall was opened daily and put on fortnightly troop entertainments and concerts, as did the Moot Hall, the borough organist playing the national anthems of all the allies on the hall's large organ and leading the mass singing of *Tipperary*. At Christmas 1914 they even mustered a choir and orchestra to sing pieces from The Messiah. The music hall attached to the Gaiety Pub on

The impressive Soldiers' Home on Queen Street from the rear.

A meal for wounded soldiers inside the Public Hall.

Mersea Road flourished; the local cinemas, the Hippodrome in High Street and the theatre in Queen Street all ran programmes featuring war-related heroics.

The largest and most central club for soldiers was the St George's Hall, the former Public Hall, set behind that other important hub, the Albert School. For eighteen years the Hall had been used by Club St George, a young men's guild which, under its founder Geoffrey Elwes, by now a leading figure in the Boy Scouts, had founded the 1st Colchester Troop. By 1915 it was being used by over 200 soldiers a night; by 1917 it was recording 25-30,000 visits a week, kept going by almost 200 volunteers and selling an immense quantity of food. Its enterprising management even installed thirteen (very cramped) slipper baths, used by over 150 men a day. This was augmented by a programme of 'bath billeting' whereby Kitchener recruits could use baths in people's homes, a luxury which only the middle classes of Colchester enjoyed in 1914.

Equally active was the YMCA, under the banner SCA (Soldier's Christian Association) who built large recreation tents at Severalls,

Mile End and Reed Hall, later replacing them with two large wooden huts at Reed Hall, one at Severalls and one at Mile End, each fitted up with platform, piano, refreshment bar, tables and chairs. They also opened two smaller premises in central Colchester. In one of his last acts as mayor, Wilson Marriage had details of all the clubs printed in a booklet, which was distributed by Boy Scouts to all households billeting soldiers. There were of course entertainment facilities in the garrison too. The music hall at Meeanee Barracks hosted boxing contests; the large Garrison gymnasium was reborn as the Garrison Variety Theatre and continued to flourish throughout the war. Professional artists came down from London to perform. It was even a two-way process. Out at Wivenhoe the Field Ambulance Unit based at Ballast Quay put on a show to entertain the locals.

This roll call of communal response must also include the devotional church. Despite compulsory church parade every Sunday morning, large numbers of recruits also attended Sunday evening church and chapel services just as they probably did back home. Understandably, each denomination reached out to their own. After one evening service at St Peter's, attended, it was claimed, by 5-600 troops, cards were distributed to any who were members of the Church of England Men's Society, inviting them all to a social. In similar manner

One of the Colchester SCA huts.

Inside one of the YMCA huts.

the Chief Scout, Lord Baden-Powell, who had been stationed as a young officer at Colchester, returned to a Moot Hall reception to address some of the 500 scout masters and former scouts now training to be soldiers here. It was a solemn occasion. 'Many of you will have to lay down your lives', announced Baden-Powell, 'and you will do it not with any grudging, but with a thrill of delight that you can show an example to other men how to die like an English gentleman.' Christian manliness? Remove the class overtones and it recalls the cry of the jihadi.

For these ex-scouts boxing and gymnastic classes were held in the scout-owned Bunting Rooms in Culver Street. Though league football ceased and Layer Road Football Ground was set aside for Army drill, a Colchester Military Football League flourished throughout the war, keeping pitches on the Abbey Field and the Recreation Ground in regular use. The presence of the Manchester Regiment in December 1916 produced a crowd of 3,000 to watch a rugby match on Abbey Field between Australia and the Manchester Regiment in which several international players took part.

The success of the community's engagement with the new army in their midst is encapsulated in the official report of Colchester's Medical Officer of Health issued in the summer of 1915. In the previous twelve months, he claimed, the borough had had only two prosecutions for drunkenness and no cases of 'war babies' from the largest concentration of soldiers that Colchester had ever seen. Given the town's reputation for much of the previous forty years, these are extraordinary, if selective, statistics. They do not for example mention cases of minor affray and petty theft by soldiers who had come before the local courts. Nor would this last. Incidence of venereal disease increased alarmingly in the army, not least from the services of French brothels on the Western Front. Not by accident were condoms called French letters throughout two world wars. In 1917, by which time most soldiers in training were conscripts, more than 10 per cent of live births in Colchester were illegitimate.

Meanwhile the Abbey Field was a sea of activity as recruits pursued the serious business of training. Fitness was secured with 'Swedish drill' – lots of knees bending, arms stretching and press-ups. Above all, the men marched everywhere, all over Colchester, out into the country, even to Clacton and back, invariably pursued by a scatter of small boys.

Soldiers under training on the Abbey Field with the Reed Hall huts to their rear.

Fitness training in the garrison gym.

They drilled in Castle Park; they drilled in Kings Head Meadow. Grass was flattened, trenches dug, and bayonets thrust into sacks packed with straw. On the outbreak of war, with harvest in progress, heavy horses and mules from all over Essex were requisitioned for war service. Hundreds churned up the Abbey Field. Many died that winter at Middlewick under the Army's 'toughening up' regime. Lorries, requisitioned complete with their solid rubber types, stood in rows. Gun carriages drawn by horses went round and round in circles. Colchester civilians came and watched in their hundreds, as they did at New Town where part of the recreation ground became a working bakery, where horses were trained and trenches were dug for simulated bayonet charges.

In November 1914 the King, George V, paid a much-publicised visit to Colchester to inspect the Norfolk and Suffolk Territorials on Braiswick Golf Course, shaking hands with several men from his own Sandringham Estate. Crowds gathered on North Hill expecting him to

Garrison farriers were kept busy shoeing several thousand horses.

proceed to the garrison but were disappointed. He left by train after an hour amid groundless speculation that problems caused by laying wood blocks in Head Street had foreshortened his trip and prevented a royal visit to the town. He was to pay two further visits to Colchester before the war ended.

In April 1915 a tragedy occurred not far from the golf course. An area on Bergholt Road was set aside for the Royal Engineers to practice tunnelling, a refinement to trench warfare. A mine was detonated in a tunnel to create a crater. All it created was loosened earth and sappers were sent in to move this away, with orders not to enter the mine chamber. Sapper Williams did, and when he did not return, four more went down to find him and got stuck too. They were rescued, but Williams was not. Second Lieutenant Darton now went in, but did not return either. Both he and Williams had been gassed by the lighter-than-air carbon monoxide released by the explosion. Eleven sappers and officers received Royal Humane Society medals for their efforts to rescue these two and the four other men.

By spring 1915 the flow of new recruits from the Colchester district was falling away, as it did across the nation, despite the efforts of the

*On Colchester Golf Course King George V shakes hand with Captain Beck,
the agent on his Sandringham Estate, serving with the Norfolk Regiment.*

local press to keep up the momentum. In December 1914 the *Essex
County Standard* had announced that 11 per cent of Mersea men were
in the forces, allegedly a British record. The figure for Colchester was
3 per cent. The new mayor, William Coats-Hutton, felt bound to say,
'Colchester has done very much worse than many other towns in
Britain.' Audiences at recruitment meetings were soon being described
as 'dismally small', now that their novelty had worn off and their
message was well known. Apart from the usual official enthusiasts,
few came. Captain Norman, in charge of local recruitment, went onto
the attack. 'I went into a grocer's shop and was served by a man big
enough to bayonet five Germans,' he announced. 'There are men who
prefer to earn their 30, 40 or 50 shillings at Paxman's... to enlisting in
this great hour of need.'

In fact, as he spoke, over 200 of Paxman's 800 peacetime workforce
were already in uniform, many having been in the local Territorials.
Indeed Colchester's recruitment slowdown can be explained as much
by the large numbers in the pre-war Reserves and Territorials as by the

current full employment in the town. Nevertheless, a recruitment march round Essex by those very Territorials, now the 5th Essex Regiment, attracted little response when they held a string of open-air recruitment meetings at East Mill, St Botolph's Corner, Colchester High Street, Lexden and Stanway. In a garrison town, the supposed glamour of military life cut little ice, while the regular arrival of the wounded at St Botolph's Station left little doubt about the reality of war. Indeed, when conscription was finally adopted, the safety of a 'reserved occupation', which Paxman employees enjoyed, was so welcome that, despite rising inflation, younger men at Paxman's were discouraged from asking for a pay rise in case they lost their jobs and became eligible for the forces. It is a necessary reminder that by 1915 Colchester and Britain was running short of patriotic young men ready to die for King and Country.

And 1915 would also be the year when twentieth-century warfare reached Colchester. Hostilities no longer took place in distant lands alone, as we will now see.

CHAPTER 4

The Defence of the Town

Sunday, 21 February 1915 was a moonlit night. At 8.50 pm a German pilot, Lieutenant Prondzynski, looked down on central Colchester, electric light visible from its restaurants, electric trams rumbling down its High Street as the last worshippers walked home from evening service. Just short of the town's well-lit artillery barracks, he carefully lifted a bomb from his open cockpit and dropped it over the side. Whether Colchester Garrison was his real target we do not know, for he had already dropped three high-explosive bombs from his Taube monoplane, two at Braintree, one at Coggeshall, all landing harmlessly in fields. His fourth bomb spun unerringly down, landing 'by Providence', as the press report said, not on the roof, but in the tiny back garden of 41, Butt Road, home of Quartermaster Sergeant Rabjohn of the 20th Hussars, his wife and their 13-month-old daughter.

A Taube plane, similar to the one that dropped the Butt Road bomb.

With the baby in bed, the Rabjohns were in their sitting room preparing to eat supper when there was 'a terrific explosion'. Behind them the kitchen was wrecked, as crockery smashed, blast hit the walls, furniture leapt, and dust filled the air. The back door blew in. Bomb shrapnel peppered the back wall of the house and shot clean through the back door, even penetrating a nine-inch thick wall to the room where the Robjohns stood. The gas mantle shattered, plunging the room into darkness. Blinded by dust, Sergeant Rabjohn turned off the gas before he and his wife stumbled upstairs to find their daughter peacefully asleep in her bed.

Outside, the bomb left a shallow crater five feet across. Outhouses collapsed under shrapnel and blast. Branches were sliced off a neighbour's tree and other houses had their back doors blown in. Windows and window frames were smashed, even some windows 75 metres away. Several residents had narrow escapes from flying glass, and goods on the shelves of Mrs Dickens's corner shop flew everywhere. Telephone wires came down, and, despite the mayor's instructions to hide in a cupboard in the event of a bomb, many people ran into the streets on hearing the explosion. Crowds gathered in Butt Road as the police arrived. Between 10 pm and midnight hundreds of volunteer troops returning from weekend leave came to have a look. The only casualty, found in the debris, was a dead thrush.

Neighbours view the devastation at 41 Butt Road.

Soldiers now guard the back garden in Butt Road. The pram has appeared.

The event attracted a great deal of media attention. An extensive account, 120 column inches long, appeared in the *Essex County Standard*, illustrated by seven photographs. The enterprising Oscar Way rushed out a postcard showing four of his photographs. It was soon selling like hot cakes both to locals and to soldiers billeted in the town. The same morning Pathé News and several national dailies arrived by train from London and descended on No 41, while enterprising neighbours overlooking the Rabjohns' back garden made 'a few bob' charging the curious 1d a view.

No. 41 was a small house. The baby's pram was kept outside in a shed whose roof had collapsed. The Robjohns had removed the pram to check its damage when the press arrived. Most of the press photographs included the pram, though in a different position on each occasion. It had clearly been moved around to 'get it in the picture'. The Pathé film opens dramatically by panning to a slightly battered pram, placed woefully on end. It had not taken journalists long to spot a storyline: the current demonisation of the Germans as 'baby killers',

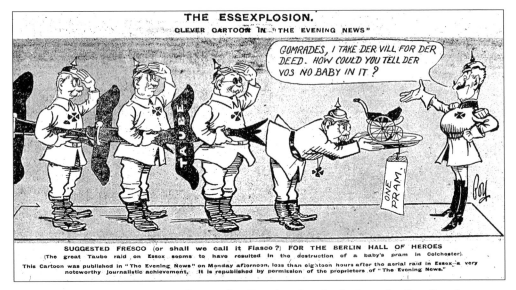

Cartoon appearing in the London Evening Standard *about the Butt Road bomb.*

a term coined by Winston Churchill following the naval bombardment of Scarborough, Whitby and Hartlepool in December 1914 where 137 people, including several children, had been killed.

One press account claimed the pram was 'smashed to atoms'. Before long a story developed that the baby could so easily have been in it. A suitably ambiguous cartoon appeared in the *London Evening News*. The *Daily Mirror* was more direct. Its headline announced, 'Sky pirates fail to kill a single baby'. Reading the *Daily Mail* version, Lady Colebrook telephoned to say that as the baby looked charming she would present a new perambulator. She ordered one from Harrods (where else?) and it arrived, along with an *Essex County Standard* reporter, at Mrs Rabjohn's door, which she opened, holding her baby. He reported that

> *'All smiles and breathless she said, 'It is kind of the lady now – Lady Colebrook did you say? It's more than kind isn't it, babs. Please say how pleased we are....' and 'babs' smiled and seemed to understand.'*

Such modern journalism was pretty advanced for the rather staid *Essex County Standard*.

The Butt Road bomb was a dramatic encouragement to improve the measures already in place against an air attack. The initiative for this came, once more, from central government, but its implementation was down to Colchester. The initial concern had been that the district would suffer a naval attack, a concern reinforced by the attacks on the Yorkshire coast in December. A coastal zone was established to which Colchester as a garrison town was added. Here, under the Defence of the Realm Act, street and shop lighting should be dimmed at night. This was taken sufficiently seriously for Mr Greenwood, fruiterer of High Street, to be arrested by the military for showing bright lights in December 1914. He was sentenced to seven days imprisonment, a sentence he had already served by the time his court martial took place. However, dimmed lights had not stopped the Butt Road bomber seeing the High Street below him. What the town needed was dimmer lights, or ultimately, full blackout, a situation Colchester achieved incrementally.

THE BABY KILLERS' WORK.
Quarter-Master Sergeant Rabjohn with his wife and baby girl standing amid the wreckage of their home at Colchester caused

Mr and Mrs Rabjohn pose for the press with their baby and its pram.

Matters were not helped by a rather cavalier approach by parts of the garrison. Letters to the paper complained of blazing lights from some units. In one spell early in 1916, the military committed eighty-eight lighting offences in three days, as a regime of increasingly severe blackout was imposed. This was now so total that in central Colchester kerbs on street corners were painted white to avoid pedestrians stumbling into the road. The gas company reduced its pressure, the electricity works, its output. Car lights were covered. Even to shine a torch skywards was an offence. Special constables watched eagle-eyed for householders opening their curtains at night, successfully securing the prosecution of several leading citizens. The chimes of the town hall clock were stopped at night lest they should be heard by the crews of passing Zeppelins; the bells of St Peter's Church were silenced. As raids continued, from 1916 trams too were stopped during alerts, lest sparks from their terminals were seen from above. And from September, a particularly active month for Zeppelin attacks, all road traffic was stopped as well.

An elaborate system of air raid alerts was now in place. Rockets were fired from coastal sites as Zeppelins crossed into Britain. The rockets could be observed by Special Constables stationed near the top of the town hall's 61 metre tower. By 1916 a comprehensive early warning system had been organised, with its own communications headquarters armed with radio and telephone. Airships could fly at a great height, but, large and slow moving, they had to cross the English coastline. Searchlights scoured the sky, anti-aircraft guns were positioned, and Zeppelin radios were intercepted. A series of giant concrete dishes (acoustic mirrors) lined the north-east coast of England, looking out to sea, supplying a fifteen-minute warning of approaching

Every night a Special Constable stood in the covered viewpoint below the top of the town hall tower, checking for Zeppelins.

The Electricity Station, home of the Colchester siren nicknamed DORA.

enemy airships. The chilly special on duty at the top of the town hall tower seems by 1916 to have been more interested in the state of Colchester's blackout than the detection of passing airships.

When an air raid alert reached the town hall, the public were told. Rather than sending policemen out on bicycles with placards saying 'TAKE COVER', the hooters at Colchester's main factories were sounded. Not till June 1917 was a special siren fitted to the Electricity Station in Stanwell Street. By now high-flying Gotha aeroplanes were the main menace, though none of them troubled Colchester. Nor did the new high-flying Zeppelins. The siren however had to be sounded every day to make sure that it still worked. Named 'Bellona' by a donnish civil servant, most Colchester people simply called it DORA.

One consequence of civilian bombing was the rapid growth in insurance schemes against damage by aircraft attacks. Alongside the local press reports of the Butt Road bombing were advertisements offering home insurance against bomb damage. Helpfully the paper itself proclaimed the foresight of Mrs Whitehead who lived next door to the Rabjohns and had insured her house against 'aerial bombs', under a scheme run by the *Daily News*. Three weeks earlier the town council itself had set up a committee to look into insuring their own buildings: the town hall, public library, electricity station, trams and tram depot, the water tower, sewerage works, isolation hospital and six elementary schools. The mayor enquired of the Prime Minister about possible government compensation. The answer was not reassuring and insurance was taken out, setting the Council back £500 a year, equivalent to a halfpenny rate. The town's largest factory complex, Paxman's, cost £911 a year to insure. It was a necessary but, as it turned out, unneeded expense. Only one other bomb appears to have landed in Colchester throughout the war.

On 31 March 1916, Zeppelin L.15 fresh from bombing Ipswich Docks where it caused three fatalities, reached Colchester's Hythe at 8.45 pm. Here it dropped a high explosive bomb, which landed on open land. A glass roof at Spottiswoode's the printers was shattered, as were many windows nearby, but, being night time, no one was injured in what was now the town's industrial heart. Satisfaction came with the news that on its way home L.15 was hit by an anti-aircraft (AA) gun at Purfleet, lost hydrogen and height, and fell into the sea north of Margate. One of her crew drowned; the rest became prisoners of war.

Zeppelins

Dorothy Lawrence, born 1897
I remember seeing the Zeppelins come over Colchester. We used to stand on the doorstep and watch them going towards London. They didn't frighten us; we just used to watch them.

Ivy Green, born 1906
I can remember the L33 Zeppelin coming down at Wigborough. My father managed to get a piece of it and had it made into brooches for us.

An amateur photo of a Zeppelin over Magdalen Street, Colchester.

Though only two bombs were dropped, hundreds of air raids warnings occurred. Each one mobilised a duty of emergency firemen, established by the borough council from former firemen, various private fire bodies and the military. By the end of the war they had been on call, usually from 11 pm till daybreak, on over 200 occasions. Zeppelins were now regularly sighted even in daylight hours. At one point in September 1916 five sat menacing over Colchester for two hours, presumably regrouping, for no bombs were dropped. The main target of their

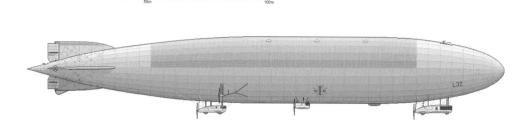

A measured drawing of the L32 super Zeppelin, twin to the one grounded at Wigborough.

attacks was now London, and Zeppelins fleeing back home, sometimes crippled by gunfire, added spice to local news, now so heavily censored that the second Colchester bomb got no press mention at all. In consequence Colchester's Zeppelin 'memory' rests more on the dramatic midnight events at the village of Little Wigborough on 23 September 1916.

Faced with the increasing ability of the allies to cripple or destroy the existing Zeppelin fleet, Germany had invested in the R class 'Super-Zeppelin'. These giant machines were 200 metres long (two football pitches) and the size of a battleship. Their lightweight aluminium frame still weighed 50 tons. Within their envelope was 2million cubic feet of inflammable hydrogen gas. Four gondolas hung below the balloon, carrying twenty-two crew, eight guns, 2,000 gallons of petrol and up to sixty bombs. With six engines, each R class cost an eye-watering £250,000. In terms of economic worth that is £94million today.

On 23 September, Germany launched an eleven-airship attack on London, which included four of the five R Class Zeppelins then built. It proved an expensive night: only one returned home. One, intercepted by a British plane, exploded in flames in North London; another suffered the same fate near Billericay in Essex; a third, L 33, dropped its bombs in Woolwich and West Ham, killing eleven people. Returning, it was caught by artillery fire. Its gas-filled bags were punctured and the main propeller disabled. It began to lose height. Reaching the coast at rooftop level, it offloaded its heavy equipment and successfully crash-landed on Copt Hall Lane, Little Wigborough, not far from the church.

The family from the cottage, who the German pilot tried to alert.

The Commander decided to destroy his airship, and knocked on the doors of two farmhouses to warn them. Terrified, they would not open their doors. The vast and valuable airship was now ignited. It was 1 am and the blaze was visible for miles. As the Commander, Böcker, marched his twenty-one men off to surrender in Colchester, he met a local special coming to check the blaze. Unfazed by twenty-two unknown men marching towards him at 1 am, the special asked 'What's on?'. In perfect English Böcker asked him the way to Colchester. 'It's some miles away', he replied, but, noting 'a foreign accent' the special was 'suspicious' and, soon joined by another special and a policeman in the area on holiday, the three followed the men to Peldon Post Office. Here the resident policeman, Constable Smith, and the village postmistress, were trying to ring Colchester Garrison to get advice. Refusing Böcker's request to use the phone, he promptly arrested them all.

A contemporary drawing of Special Constable Nicholas leading the L33 crew to Mersea.

Other specials arrived to march the crew over the Strood to West Mersea where they spent the night under guard. News of what had happened spread far and wide. Even the press felt able to cover it, carefully avoiding all reference to place names. Constable Smith, who arrested Captain Bocker (and refused his request to use the telephone), was promoted to sergeant. The posse of specials who escorted the Germans to Mersea received gold watches and newspaper praise. But residents of this maritime community knew better: the enterprise had been less heroic, more 'Dad's Army'. Sergeant Smith was forever known as Zepp Smith.

The huge aluminium skeleton of L33 now lay like a beached whale across a road and two fields. Although it was 12 miles away by road, a considerable percentage of Colchester's population managed to go and see it. This was the age of the bicycle. The Army hastily organised some crowd control but not before souvenir hunters had started to help themselves to fragments of the aluminium struts. Military cordons did not entirely halt this pillage – there was a lot of aluminium. Before long, aluminium charms and tokens, allegedly made from molten struts, appeared for sale: they can still be sourced online today. Donations levied at the site raised £74 for the Red Cross. A convoy of cars took 100 wounded soldiers to see it all. The site was filmed and

The giant skeleton of L33 guarded by the military.

The special team sent to examine and dismantle L33.

shown to full houses at the enterprising Vaudeville Cinema on St Botolph's Corner, and later in London cinemas.

Fourteen weeks later a team of naval experts came to study the Zeppelin's frame, cut it up and disposed of the aluminium. Aspects of its advanced design were incorporated into post-war UK airships. By this date it was calculated that 250,000 people from far and wide had visited the site.

Another reminder of civilian jeopardy was the plan to evacuate Colchester in the event of a German invasion. For this, as in all else, the government took the lead. Tiers of emergency committees were set up, starting with a Central County Committee. The one for Essex met in October 1914, chaired by the Lord Lieutenant and dominated by the military. It was decided that, in the event of invasion, threatened Essex communities would decamp *en masse* to Oxfordshire. A Colchester Emergency Committee now met, chaired by the mayor. This in turn liaised with a range of village committees from the area covered by the evacuation plans: the Tendring Hundred, rural Lexden & Winstree and the Witham area. From the outset Colchester had misgivings about the county plans, specifically the proposed evacuation routes, which followed very narrow lanes. This was in fact deliberate, in order to leave 'main' roads free for the military to move troops to the coast against the invading army.

Colchester's protest was dismissed and in January 1915 every household received a letter from the mayor explaining the evacuation plans and a household card, colour-coded by ward, specifying the route to be followed. A rocket would be fired from the town hall tower to alert the population to leave, followed by three rockets sent up at regular intervals and the ringing of church bells meaning 'depart immediately'. The route to be followed was very specific. For those in north and east Colchester the destination was Great Bradley in Suffolk, a distance of 33 miles. This was to be reached in two days but, as the card helpfully said, '*it is recognised that some people will not be able to walk 5 miles in one journey*'. Quite how up to 10,000 people would be accommodated in Great Bradley, population 230, and quite how they then got to Oxfordshire, was unclear.

Dialogue continued and in May 1916, the coloured cards were replaced by identically coloured cards with revised instructions. The town hall rockets disappeared because '*by order of the Military*

Borough of Colchester.

INSTRUCTIONS ISSUED BY THE EMERGENCY COMMITTEE.

January, 1915.

Please insert your name and address here.
{ Name ....

{ Address..

This card must be carefully kept, as it shows you what to do if the Military Authorities give an order that everybody is to leave Colchester.

If the Order is given, you will be notified by Signal. The Signal will be as follows :—

1. To prepare to leave :—One rocket sent up from the Town Hall Tower. This signal will be given three times at intervals of five minutes.

2. To leave the Town :—Three rockets sent up from the Town Hall Tower. This signal will be given three times at intervals of five minutes, and Church Bells will be rung.

If the last Signal only should be given, it would mean that you must leave the Town without any delay ; and you should if possible take with you enough food for yourself and your family for 48 hours.

You are told on the back of this card (**which you must take with you**) the direction you are to follow and by which roads you must go.

The card sent to all Colchester residents with evacuation instructions.

Authorities no sound or other signal is permitted'. Instead 40,000 inhabitants would now be alerted to flee by pasting a special red poster all over the town. The new cards advised of new destinations. North and east Colchester would now travel 40 miles to Saffron Walden also in Essex; those in the south to Bishop's Stortford in Hertfordshire. Each local village involved in the evacuation received similar instructions,

Special Constables wearing their armbands. This group escorted the Zeppelin crew to Mersea.

each with its own route west. How they would all get to Oxfordshire was still not stated, though those in authority had been told that passage through Hertfordshire would be organised by Hertfordshire's Emergency Committees.

In both Colchester and the villages special constables would play a key role, organising the evacuation. As ever, community leaders would lead. The Lexden & Winstree Emergency Committee was chaired by the Hon. James Round of Birch Hall, the former MP, now the Chief Superintendent of Special Constables for Lexden & Winstree. The Secretary was Charles Gooch of Wivenhoe Park, now the Superintendent of Special Constables. In Colchester it was the mayor.

Inevitably, some village authorities struggled to cope with the evacuation orders, not least the requirement that all supplies of grain, hay, straw and, above all, livestock were to be destroyed before leaving. How hundreds of cows, pigs, sheep and horses were to be killed in so short a space of time and how much notice would be taken, when some farmers were frankly uncooperative, concerned them. It was the view of the County Committee that the answer was hours, not days.

The new coloured cards required all households to take with them

REVISED ROUTES.

East Ward

Inhabitants in St. Leonard's Polling District to proceed via

Back Lane
The Moors
Brook Street
East Hill to
West Bergholt
and then as North Ward Route

Inhabitants in Kendall Road Polling District to proceed via

Wimpole Road
Brook Street
East Hill to
West Bergholt
and then as North Ward Route

Inhabitants in St. James' and Parson's Heath Polling District to proceed via

East Hill
Roman Road
Castle Road
Serpentine Walk
North Station Road
Bergholt Road to
West Bergholt
and then as North Ward Route

North Ward via

West Bergholt
Fordham
Rochfords
Mount Bures
Alphamstone
Wickham St. Pauls
Great Yeldham
Toppesfield
Robinhood End
Cornishall End
Gt. Samford
Little Brockholds
Upper Green
Cole End
Beare Hall
Saffron Walden

The revised card of the evacuation route from Colchester to Saffron Walden.

'*enough food for yourself and your family for 48 hours*'. They were to travel in groups of fifty to seventy, billeted in villages en route. The Colchester Committee replied that it could not undertake to organise up to 50,000 people into groups of fifty. They also pointed out that almost all motor vehicles in Colchester were to be requisitioned by the Army. How would the immobile travel? Would they be carried? Could one be confident that children, the elderly, the less active or unfit could walk the 40 miles to Saffron Walden in two days? And what were hordes to eat when they got to Saffron Walden, given that the villages of Lexden and Winstree were heading there too?

Answers to these questions were not encouraging: people should take as much money as possible in order to buy food; the immobile would probably have to travel on farm carts or be left behind; those in hospitals, asylums and workhouses would only be taken in the unlikely event that there was *'sufficient notice and train transport was available'*. Meanwhile the basement of Colchester Town Hall was crammed from floor to ceiling with tins of cocoa and biscuits to fortify the citizens of Clacton and Frinton when they arrived, fleeing the invading army.

We cannot be sure of the impact on Colchester's residents of getting these coloured cards with their strident messages. This was a society used to obeying orders, even as Colchester's leading lights were used to giving them. The press was quick to note residents buying perambulators to carry their food (and their children) on the long walk, even having one packed and ready in an outhouse, but preparation for evacuation is never mentioned by surviving oral history. At most, like Zeppelin attacks, it simply became part of the growing aggravation of daily wartime life.

Fortunately the coloured cards were never put to the test. Just four months later, as Colchester flocked to see the skeleton of the Wigborough Zeppelin, the Home Office had second thoughts. The local papers announced in a large block advertisement issued by the mayor: 'In the event of invasion remain in your homes. Do not follow the instructions given. These should be destroyed.' Even this ruling did not last. In March 1917 it was rescinded and officialdom informed that 'In case of invasion all those who desire to move can do so', following the routes previously outlined. As we all know, this never became necessary. Its only legacy was a series of boards bearing arrows, nailed to trees along the routes, a few of which were still there ten years later. However, at the time it caused alarm. At Tiptree's jam factory Mr Wilkin's Tiptree Hall housed a military unit. At 1 am on 25 March an invasion alert was received and the military left with their guns and baggage for the coast. Mr Wilkin hurriedly hid vital papers and told villagers they were off to Oxfordshire, and the factory was to be destroyed in the event of an invasion. Only later did he discover it was only a test mobilisation.

PRIVATE.
(Original Pattern.)

OFFICER.
(The Rank Mark is that of a
Company Commander.)

PRIVATE.
(Permissible Alternative Style.)

UNIFORMS.

The much desired uniform of the Colchester Volunteer Corps.

An evolving plan for civilian evacuation was not the only response to the threat of invasion. There was the Volunteer Corps. In the heady days of August 1914, with the local football league suspended, members of Colchester Town Football Club, led by their Secretary, Charles Clark, voted to use their ground at Layer Road for drilling by a proposed Athletes Volunteer Corps for men over 35, too old for military service. At the same time William Paxman, son of James, a former Captain of the old Volunteers and an expert shot, was arranging for Paxman employees over the recruiting age to become firearm proficient with rifles owned by the Grammar School Cadet Corps. A meeting was called to form a Home Defence Corps and the two men combined to provide the new group with route marches on Sundays led by Captain Paxman, even as Kitchener's Volunteers arrived in town and began doing the same thing.

Similar over-age 'Volunteer' groups sprang up all over the country. By November there was a national organisation for Volunteer Corps, recognised by the War Office. Recruitment for the Colchester Corps grew. By March 1915 it had 250 members; by May nearly 400. Eventually there were 700. This coincided with a policy to also recruit those too young for military service. They thus served, as the Territorials once had, as a source for future recruitment. Like Colchester Town Football Club, the Colchester Volunteer Corps had a distinctly middle-class feel, boosted by factory employees who saw career advantages. Like the Territorials before them they enjoyed summer camps.

Details were soon published of a War Office approved uniform, far more impressive than the armband of the specials. With lovat green jackets and breeches (khaki was forbidden) and a peaked cap, it looked like an officer's uniform. An indignant letter to a Chelmsford newspaper protested that army recruits were actually saluting the Volunteers. All ranks wore a red armband carrying in large initials G.R. (Georgius Rex – King George), though, inevitably, alternative suggestions abounded, of which 'Government Rejects' was one of the more printable. A public subscription was launched to finance Colchester's uniforms and equipment to which, despite the objection of the Ratepayers' Association, the borough council donated £250, possibly because of the presence in the ranks of that great council playmaker, Gurney Benham. Despite the demands of the war, the new uniforms were cut and tailored by Colchester's large clothing factories. Clearly the uniforms, an important psychological asset, were a priority.

Gurney Benham subsequently became Commander of the Volunteer Corps, their first Commander and Adjutant, Major Jenks and William Paxman, having left to take up commissions elsewhere. For a long time the Corps owned only one rifle, but eventually they acquired a set of short Japanese rifles. This coincided with a growing willingness by the government to see Volunteers as a viable military body. As well as marching and drilling, the Corps helped with guarding vulnerable sites, increasingly co-ordinating on a countywide basis. The logical step was to annex them to the Essex Regiment and from July 1918 they became the 6th Volunteer Battalion of the Essex Regiment, were permitted to wear khaki and were issued with army equipment. By this date numbers of special constables, though earlier forbidden, had transferred

Mr Smart, draper (left) and Mr Bird, publican, both of St Botolph's, line up with the Essex Motor Volunteer Corps, Coast Section.

to the Volunteers, often enlisting during this last year of war. There was also, for those few who owned cars or lorries, the opportunity to join (with their cars) the Essex Motor Volunteer Corps (Coast section). Had the German Spring Offensive of 1918 miraculously turned into an invasion they would have met a large and determined resistance.

Nevertheless, the contents of this chapter have little to do with winning the war; and everything to do with living in Colchester for four extraordinary years. Most people knew that Colchester was not going to face the German Army; their sons, fathers and husbands were. As casualty figures mounted this became the greater reality. And our story must move from Zeppelin excitement to the dread of War Office letters and the twice-weekly routine of watching the wounded arrive at St Botolph's Railway Station.

CHAPTER 5

One Vast Hospital

The Battle of the Somme is a terrible landmark in British history. By Christmas 1915, a line of trenches stretched from the Alps to the Sea. Stalemate engulfed the Western Front. The Allies planned to break the deadlock with an offensive at the Somme in July 1916. The Colchester papers called it The Big Push. After that we would win the war.

By the end of June, German trenches had been reinforced with a thoroughness that left our men gob-smacked when they finally overran them. Facing the Allies a double lines of barbed wire embraced an extensive minefield beyond which were a triple line of trenches linked by telephone, concrete dugouts 10 metres deep and pill boxes armed with machine guns – the Allies never equalled this. On 1 July after seven days continuous shelling of the German lines, clearly heard some 200 miles away in Colchester, the Territorials and Kitchener's Army, including a significant number of Colchester men, went 'over the top'. On Day One the British Army suffered 57,470 casualties, 19,240 fatal. Of those wounded many finished up in Colchester.

Britain threw in the Australians who suffered 'the worse 24 hours in Australian history'; then the South Africans, who suffered unthinkable casualties, many just buried in mud. By Christmas, when it ended, estimated casualties totaled: British 513,000, French 434,000, German 500,000. The Allies had advanced just 5 miles, but the German Army, simultaneously suffering 434,000 casualties at Verdun, had retreated; no one had 'won'. The battle of attrition would continue. And Colchester was one vast hospital.

A Somme Offensive trench.

THE BIG PUSH

Charles Herbert, born 1897

I joined up in High Street one Saturday morning and by dinner time I was at Warley [Barracks]. After I went to France my first battle was at Arras. We went over the top on Easter Monday; that's when almost all of our Essex Yeomanry got killed. We followed them over and after we'd had a good many days battling there, as luck would have it, I came out all right. We came back to the trenches again and then shifted onto the Somme. Well, we lost the Essex Cycle Battalion there; they were on our left and old Jerry surrounded them....

We were up to our knees in mud and water in the trenches. It's a wonder it did not kill the lot of us. We didn't get any sleep. You couldn't sleep with that lot going on. There were Verey lights going up, and you could see old Gerry patrolling round, and there were all these shells and wiz-bangs going off....

We used to go out on night patrols to try and destroy Jerry's pill boxes.... We would go through the barbed wire carrying about 13 bombs in a bag and when we got near enough we would throw them into the entrance. They'd be nearly finished by the time we got there, and those that weren't – well you were told not to bring any prisoners. Those that were alive would be finished off....

And from there, just as I'd been fighting, I came home on leave. When I got home I had to go out in the shed and have a bath – I was absolutely lousy. You'd never seen so many lice in your life.

Bob Hewes, born 1897

I'm a lucky man to be alive. We were in action... and we overran the front line between our line and the German line. And in between were little slit trenches what held about 3 men. Well, 3 of us jumped into one under heavy bombardment. One of them who'd been there on Observation knew how to get back so he nipped back. We two stopped in there and some German officer came out of a dugout and was right on to us. He shot the other bloke and he fell down dead, poor bloke. I saw he'd got this rifle – and he weren't further away than that door – and he aimed it and I thought, 'that's yer lot, say your prayers boy; that's it'. Anyway, he fired again and I knew I weren't dead: I was still conscious. Fact, I wondered where he'd hit me 'cos I went down. And he'd hit my foot. Anyway, I couldn't get away... I always reckon that man had a heart. He perhaps had boys of his own. He thought, 'he's only a boy, I'll just wing him' – y'know? So I was a prisoner...

I can honestly say I was decently treated by the Germans.

As a garrison town, close to the continent and the continental port of Harwich, Colchester was from the outset a reception centre for the wounded. Long before 1916 the arrival of casualties at St Botolph's Station took on a standard pattern. The first trainload, late in the evening of 24 September 1914, was a major Colchester event, carefully

Members of the Essex Cycle Brigade parading in a snowy cavalry barracks early in 1916.

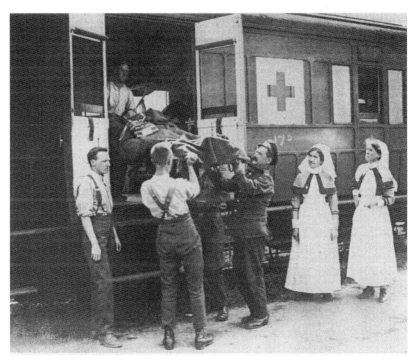

A stretcher case leaving the hospital train.

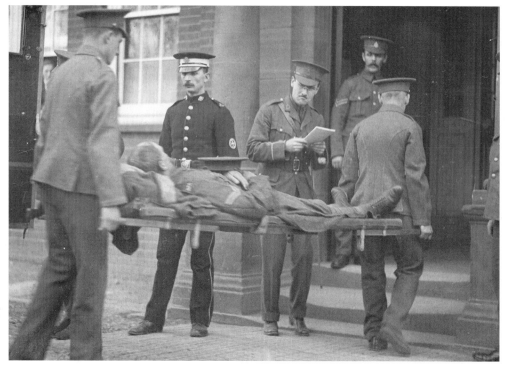

A stretcher case being assessed on arrival at the Military Hospital.

recorded in the press. Large crowds gathered to watch a nine carriage train carrying ninety-four men and one officer pull into the station to be met by a line of Red Cross nurses, St John's Ambulance with its horse ambulance, and a fleet of assorted cars, supplied by residents.

The mayor of Colchester, Wilson Marriage, escorted the first five casualties to his car, as his daughter presented them with a bunch of home-grown grapes. The men looked 'solemn and perplexed' the press observed, as well they might: they weren't from the Western Front but from Egypt, and only two of the ninety-five casualties actually needed a stretcher. 'Thousands' lined the route to the Military Hospital and every car was cheered as it went by. This scene was repeated twice a week for the next four years. Over time the crowd became more active. Sweets were thrown at the walking wounded and cigarettes offered. And the cars always turned up. Before long they were joined by an army motor ambulance, and, in an early fund-raising effort, Colchester purchased a second. It was soon needed.

A horse ambulance practising for work at the front. In Colchester only two horses were used.

Colchester's Red Cross Motor Ambulance was paid for by public subscription.

THE WOUNDED

George Cuthew, born 1906

The wounded soon started arriving in convoy trains and were taken to the Military Hospital. The townspeople used to congregate round St Botolph's Corner and handed the wounded 'cigs' and chocolate. The Hospital was soon overflowing and they put the wounded on the floors of the Garrison Gym and the Garrison School till they got more beds. We used to go to the side doors at the Gym and the wounded, as they got better, asked us to get them cigs etc. from the shops. I was there one day and saw one poor chap die, something I remembered a long time. On Sundays the walking wounded used to walk in the hospital grounds and people used to come to the rails to talk and give them food and things.

Colchester Military Hospital, 1916

Private Wood of the Buffs was brought here suffering from shock and severe injuries sustained through being buried in a wrecked trench. He had altogether lost the power of speech and all efforts to restore it were futile. At length it was decided to send for his mother who lives in Doncaster. When Mrs Wood arrived she was ushered quietly into the ward and took up a stand at the foot of her son's bed.

After looking hard at his visitor for some time, Wood got excited and at length called out, 'Mother, Mother!' Now he is able to converse freely. He explained he was in deep distress and had tried his utmost to articulate but could not utter a word.

The Military Hospital, a lavish, modern building, could accommodate 250 patients. This rapidly proved inadequate. The war had barely started when large numbers of wounded Belgian soldiers arrived. By 1916, enhanced by a range of wooden huts and by fitting more beds in wards and corridors, the hospital could eventually house a staggering 1,800. Then came the Battle of the Somme. The military also took over the newly completed Hamilton Road Central School, converting that into additional hospital space. By the time the war ended the hospital

Colchester Military Hospital was larger than the civilian hospital on Lexden Road. (Heather Johnson collection)

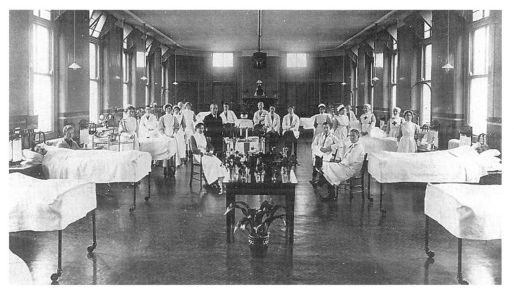

A relaxed pre-war photo of a serene military hospital ward and its staff. This would soon change. (Heather Johnson collection)

had a staff of 355 doctors, nurses, catering, administration and maintenance staff, spread across several sites. Central to their success were the Red Cross Voluntary Aid Detachment (VAD) nurses.

Colchester had begun the war with a strong Red Cross presence, focused on that middle class stronghold, Lexden Road. Major Freeman, convinced that international danger threatened, had for some time been running nurse training classes, whose graduates became approved VAD nurses. Early in 1914 the branch quartermaster, Mrs Towsey, secured the approval of the rector of St. Mary's to convert his parish room in Rawstorn Road (today an architects' office) into a hospital in the event of war. She then secured promises from willing residents to finance a bed or some necessary equipment. When war broke out the promises were duly honoured and the small hospital was equipped, until the military rightly declared its sanitary arrangement inadequate. Nothing daunted, they secured the use of the Public Hall and moved in, only to be told it was unacceptable too. Finally, they rented Gostwycke, an empty house in Cambridge Road, the former home of the Sanders family prior to its move to Lexden Park.

Gostwycke was approved and in September 1914 Gostwycke Auxiliary Hospital became an arm of the Military Hospital. With a modest number of beds, it tended well over 2,000 wounded during the war. Its matron, nurses, dispenser, quartermaster, cooks, kitchen maids and scullery helpers were a roll call of middle class ladies, an early and notable example of the part they played and the opportunities they seized during the war. Their commandant Evelyn Wren worked tirelessly till her health broke down in 1917. She would later receive an OBE. Other Colchester VADs left to work on the Western Front and in Serbia. Similar Red Cross Hospitals were also established at Stanway Rectory, the infants' school at Wivenhoe, the future Holmwood House School, and large houses at Mersea, Horkesley and Ardleigh, though not all continued throughout the war. All were very popular with troops. They were smaller, more 'homely', and the nurses were 'wonderful'. One near Clacton, dedicated to troops who had lost limbs, made the press when the men gained access to a vehicle and went on a pub crawl from which they were rescued, paralytic, by the staff.

Colchester's civilian hospital on Lexden Road, the Essex County Hospital, was equally engaged. To free up beds it moved all female patients to the Colchester High School in Wellesley Road. It then secured money to place two large wooden huts in its grounds where the wounded were treated. Finally, it erected two large canvas marquees, raising its bed total to 339, the largest it had ever been. Almost 4,000 wounded soldiers were thus housed and treated during the war. The isolation hospital at Mile End also put up additional huts,

Staff associated with Gostwycke Hospital, photographed in the back garden. The trees behind are still there. (Heather Johnson collection)

One of the two wooden 'Netley' Huts erected at the Essex County Hospital, exclusively for military cases (Colchester Medical Society).

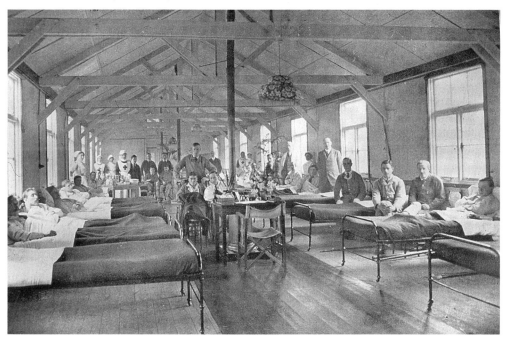

Some of the 133 nurses employed at by the Military Hospital. (Heather Johnson collection)

and, as more men emerged from the trenches suffering from shell shock, Severalls Mental Hospital admitted quite a number, though took no part in any of the pioneer treatments then being tested. Indeed, twenty-one of them, now totally institutionalised, were still there in 1957. As the war progressed the workload on all these hospitals rose and staff became very weary. The trainloads of wounded now contained many men unable to walk, suffering from 'trench foot', an unpleasant degrading of flesh when exposed to prolonged wet.

All the wounded needed dressings, bandages, splints, even substitutes for lost limbs. Increasingly the military struggled to cope, but benefitted from the provision of garments and bandages produced on an almost industrial scale by the Colchester War Work Depot, launched at the outset of war by the incoming mayoress, Mrs Coats Hutton. A meeting of leading ladies put up £50 and purchased the material. Free of charge, cutters at Turner's clothing factory cut this into garment sections for the ladies to sew up in the former art rooms of that wartime powerhouse, the Albert School. Within weeks they received an urgent appeal from the Military Hospital: their Red Cross store was down to just two bed jackets and one pair of socks.

The work of the depot expanded, from one room to several, from a few to fifty seamstresses, from one day a week to six – and all day long, sometimes into the night. Skills were developed: Mrs Paxman, wife of the captain, specialised in padded splints. Next, satellite sewing groups were formed all round the town. Churches, cub scouts, schoolchildren and workplaces were enlisted: twenty-four groups in all. There was a Dedham & Stour Valley outpost. Links were even forged with a War Work Depot in Taunton, Somerset. Increased fundraising followed to buy materials, which soon cost over £1,000 a year (£71,000 now). And in order to be free to send their products where they thought best, Colchester did not join any government scheme. As well as to the Military Hospital, robes and bandages were sent to prisoners of war, to the Dardanelles, to the French wounded, to Serbian Relief, to the Military Hospital at Ipswich, to the Mission to Seamen and to Colchester men serving abroad: hundreds of thousands of garments, thousands of miles of bandages.

In just one year their output for the Military Hospital alone included: c.14,000 garments, 22,488 roller bandages, 14,976 plugs, 6,384 washing gloves, 1,620 triangular bandages, 414 eye pads, 449 arm splints, 420 T-bandages, 122 head bandages, 92 stump and shoulder

The arrival of wounded Belgians at the Military Hospital in 1914, wearing their luggage labels. (Heather Johnson collection)

bandages, 160 webbing slings, 120 'helpless case' shirts, 156 chloroform & theatre masks…. The full list is far too long to include, but with the thoroughness of enthusiasm, someone carefully recorded those precise numbers. Did it help the hospital? Undoubtedly. Was it exhilarating? Probably. What we should reflect on is the transforming effect this mass organisation had on an unknown number of women, not yet able to vote, used to supervising servants, to deferring to their men, to exchanging visiting cards, to ordering the groceries or dressing up for Sunday morning church, activities which doubtless continued alongside this great endeavour.

Mrs Coats Hutton.   *Mrs Slaughter.*   *Mr Wicks.*

Nor was this the only organisation established by Colchester women. Women also took the lead in providing 'comforts', invariably things to eat, for soldiers in the various hospitals and those troops arriving or departing at Colchester's North Station. The former was led by Mrs Slaughter who at the request of the Colonel in charge of the Military Hospital initiated her Basket Fund. Nine large baskets toured the wards with sweets, cigarettes, chocolate, toiletries, newspapers – a sort of mobile shop whose produce was free. This operation was financed, like so much wartime charity work in Colchester, by a range of concerts, shows, door-to-door canvassing and subscription lists. Increasingly Mrs Slaughter's initiative became a major operation costing £600 a year, with eighteen baskets circulating and thirty helpers touring the wards of the various hospitals, offering at the same time

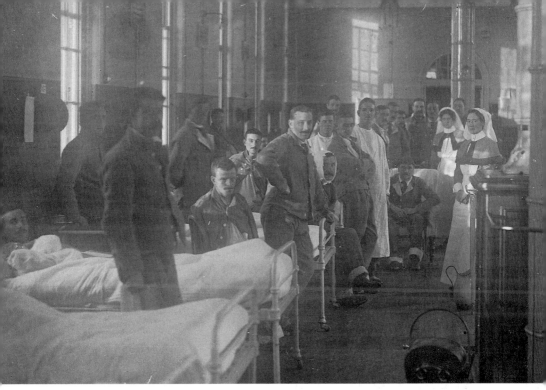

Overcrowded wards soon became normal at the Military Hospital (Colchester & Ipswich Museum Service).

perhaps its most important contribution: a human face and a chance to talk.

Up at North Station the stationmaster, Mr Wicks, partly at his own expense, provided a free buffet, cigarettes and newspapers to men being drafted overseas. Eventually this became a more structured arrangement supported by the War Office, funded by subscriptions solicited by Colchester women, and sometimes by individual officers paying for a meal for their troops in the station refreshment room. A Free Buffet for the Wounded was simultaneously operated for incoming ambulance trains. Some 17,000 troops benefitted overall.

The Soldiers' Laundry and Mending Guild started informally early in the war with Miss Lander personally mending soldiers' clothing. The arrival of Kitchener's Army with only the clothes they stood up in, greatly increased her work, particularly in coping with disintegrating boots and bruised feet after days of route marching. She wrote to friends, solicited help, and assembled women to do clothes washing as well as mending. A fee was charged, all of which went to the women washers who, often from struggling households, were thereby beneficiaries of a useful income. Eventually there were eleven branches of the Guild in each of which thirty to forty women washed twenty to thirty bundles a night, meeting the collective needs of 1,200 men a day. The large mending groups, recruited from all strata of society, gave of their time freely and made no charge for their work. This extraordinary organisation was thus not just an example of entrepreneurial drive but an outlet for *service*, not to say shared endeavour, which, provided at a time of national need, was profoundly fulfilling. Frances Lander's own reflections cannot be bettered:

> *But for the cruelty of war, these times were worth living in, and I would be most grateful for such another opportunity for service. In our work we were united and <u>happy</u>, and we stood solid for the cause we had in hand and for me to say the men appreciated our help is, I feel, but poorly to express the gratitude they tried so constantly to show – not that we wished for thanks: what we were doing was our joyous duty.*

Such ad hoc charitable activity was widespread in Colchester, as it was in the nation. Concerts, dances, sales of produce and sales of work, many organised through, or in, church premises, proliferated. All thirty-five rest rooms for soldiers needed funding. One wartime mayor, John Bailey, launched a successful appeal for £500 (£31,000 today) for the work of the YMCA among troops. The Ladies Committee of War Workers solicited money to send a parcel of food valued at twelve shillings every week to every known Colchester prisoner of war. And, it should be noted, most of these parcels arrived. Weekly street collections, often taking the form of selling 'flags': small paper symbols, held by a pin to go on the lapel of a coat, abounded. Such were their number, that from 1915 the town council issued licences to each one in turn: Belgium refugees, destitute Serbians, Red Cross supplies… the list was considerable.

Perhaps the least recognised work of Colchester women throughout the war was with the wives and families of soldiers. We have already seen in Chapter 1 the pre-war problems facing army wives who were not 'on the strength', and who were left potentially destitute if a regiment went overseas. It was a problem that had confronted the local Sailors' and Soldiers' Families Association (SSFA) when in 1914 the garrison had left for France and they sought to trace all cases of local distress. Help came from the Colchester branch of the Charity Organisation Society (COS), which had long operated a system of women district visitors, dividing Colchester into nine districts. Led by Catherine Hunt, wife of a Lexden Road doctor and daughter of a former mayor, advised by a committee made up of one woman from each district, they soon compiled a comprehensive list of all wives and families off the strength across Colchester, setting up an Enquiry Office in, yet again, the old Albert School.

Dame Catherine Hunt wearing her order.

As we have seen in Chapter 2 financial help to those in distress was provided by the Prince of Wales Fund, but this took time to organise, let alone disburse. From 10 am to 6 pm streams of forlorn army wives arrived at the Albert School to register and seek help. It fell to Catherine Hunt and her team to give financial advances pending the arrival of public funds. In September came the order to evacuate the garrison's married quarters to accommodate those training Kitchener's Volunteers. This included those officers' wives who ran the SSFA. Catherine Hunt took over the Secretaryship, issuing furnishing grants for wives to set up home elsewhere. Some wives went back to India and South Africa. Help was needed to sort out their finances too. Soldiers' wives were not always expert at paperwork and the details were complex. The Enquiry Office advised, helped with correspondence, and conducted correspondence if they thought the authority's calculations wrong. This support and advocacy continued throughout the war.

Soon the first casualty details arrived. It now fell to district visitors to offer practical support and bereavement counselling to some wives and children. Widows' pensions needed explaining, calculating and securing. Young orphan children might be transferred to aunts or grandparents. Next came the stream of wounded and discharged men, consigned to the scrapyards of Blighty, adjusting to flash-backs, to feeling a failure, to finding alternative employment in a time of war;

to family adjustment. Many needed on-going medical treatment, another issue where finance, bureaucracy and advocacy intermixed. Unsurprisingly, what was later termed marriage guidance was needed too, as couples went through stress barriers in an era when separation, let alone divorce, was socially unacceptable and financially disastrous. And this was a social service operation run by untrained, sometimes young, women volunteers. Nor should we ignore its contribution to maintaining social cohesion in a time when class hostility could easily have erupted.

As the war ground on, the rising number of dead increased the workload. The rules, and therefore the small print of wives' entitlement, kept changing. In 1916 the government intervened and established a Statutory Committee to handle all local claims. The new body had representatives from the town council, employers, labour, women and voluntary bodies. It was large and met monthly and was most active in dealing with the care and treatment of discharged servicemen. It lasted a year until the Ministry of Pension's War Pensions Committee replaced it. This however still left the local volunteers dealing directly with the wives and families. Nor did their labours end with the Armistice in 1918; things actually accelerated as men came home. Only in May 1920 did the office close. Appropriately in the Honours List that year Catherine Hunt was made a Dame and her Co-Secretary, Emily Digby, a CBE.

Finally, we should note that this long saga of female labour constituted unpaid work, charitable endeavour indeed, appropriate to the middle classes from which the participants came. Catherine Hunt, Emily Digby, Evelyn Wren, Frances Lander, Ethel Coats Hutton and their many earnest helpers all came from the comfortable end of Colchester society and their contributions, and that of those who laboured in the hospitals, stayed strictly within the 'women's sphere' of home-makers, cake-makers, carers. There is little here to excite the feminist. Though several had been active in pursuit of the suffrage, that project was promptly set aside in August 1914 in order to serve their country in a way culturally acceptable to the age. There were, however, a far larger number of young working women in Colchester for whom war wages loomed larger than war service. Fortunately, as we shall now see, the conflict would require their skills too.

CHAPTER 6

Manufacturing for War

By mid-1915 UK deaths on the Western Front required 10-15,000 replacements a week. But Britain was running out of new volunteers, not least when men in trades like engineering, vital to the war, were now being 'badged', i.e. made exempt from military service. The government launched a national survey of how many men, eligible for the forces, were still in work and in what trade. Implementation fell to local government. In Colchester Alderman Blaxill, though responsible for a large family firm, worked almost fulltime with a town hall clerk, 111 local teachers, sixty-nine volunteers and thirty-five boy scouts to complete the survey. All 10,000 Colchester households were visited and the government forms were explained. Those who did not return them were revisited. The forms were sorted; the details listed. It took them eleven weeks. It revealed, as expected, that numbers of non-exempt, unmarried Colchester men were still civilians.

Alderman Blaxill.

The government now launched a scheme devised by Lord Derby, the Minster of War, for such men to 'attest' their willingness to enlist, when needed. Another house-to-house canvass was set up by Blaxill to encourage men to attest. It encountered a certain amount of verbal abuse. It recorded 1,058 who had now enlisted or promised to attest;

645 who claimed to be unfit for service, 105 whose employer would not release them, 202 whose forms, for various reasons, were invalid and 1,260 who refused, or were unlikely, to attest. The Prime Minister now announced that married men who had attested would not be called up while any single men remained. From here it was a small step to compulsory conscription, introduced in March 1916 for all single men aged 18 to 41 and extended in May to all married men. By 1917 the bottom of that barrel was also being scraped: 36 per cent of those now left were not deemed physically capable of military service.

Conscripted recruits came to Colchester in their thousands to train, and households involved in billeting recalled that conscripted men, often older and from 'the North', were 'rough' and less personable than Kitchener's boys. By 1917 this was exacerbated by growing shortages in the shops. The shortfall in army manpower, meanwhile, was never made good. Despite raising the age of conscription to 52, by 1918 the army was smaller than it had been in 1917. But if the army was short of men, Colchester employers were even shorter.

Along with conscription came local tribunals to hear appeals by conscripts for military exemption on grounds of conscience, health or occupation. Tribunal membership consisted of town councillors,

A pre-war shot of the main Colchester Co-op with some of its many male staff.

Mr Medcalf's cycle shop made much use of teenage boys as assistants.

representatives of labour and of women, but the dominant voice in Colchester was the military spokesman, Major Howard. By 1917 Colchester Co-op, a major employer, had lost 70 per cent of its male staff. The Colchester Brewing Company (CBC) had in 1914 employed 134 men: 112 had now joined up, eighteen had failed medicals, three were too old. As well as producing beer, CBC owned 300 pubs. Naturally they appealed to the tribunal that the loss of their few remaining men would jeopardise their war effort: sustaining morale by quenching the district's thirst.

Colchester was still a town of small businesses and a few factories. Mr Archer, coal merchant, had lost fifteen of his eighteen staff, Fred Medcalf, bicycle merchant, had lost thirteen out of fourteen. Wombach's unpleasant factory at the Hythe, which degraded animal carcases, had lost thirteen out of its eighteen men and could not persuade women to work there. Sausages, a staple of British diet, all had skins made from pig intestines and Wombach's only had three elderly skin dressers left. The *Essex County Standard*, bringing the news to the district (including details of each tribunal) had lost half its male staff, many of them skilled men. And what about one-man businesses, which were quite common, particularly among shopkeepers? One consequence of labour shortages was the closure of shops at lunchtime and as early as 3 pm in winter. This was of course partly due to the introduction of blackout, as week-by-week Colchester employers pleaded their case with the tribunal to retain their dwindling staff.

Some 2,088 tribunal appeals were made in Colchester up till the Armistice in 1918. Allowing for some duplications, this must represent a large percentage of those conscripted. They were all listened to carefully, but few work-based appeals were upheld. The normal response was to delay conscription for a month or more to allow alternative arrangements to be made, often suggesting what that alternative might be. By 1918 the problem for small employers was getting so critical that a Special Traders Committee was set up 'to keep small traders going who are serving, or whose men are serving'. Meetings were held by each of the main trades: butchers, drapers, grocers etc. and these made arrangements to support any loss to conscription, often by drafting in a retired draper or grocer, to the relevant shop. In similar fashion retired teachers were now keeping many Colchester schools going, while some shopkeepers, from newsagents to barbers, illegally employed boys of school age where they could. The Colchester Tribunal was less severe, however, with the significant number of men who sought exemption because they had sole care of an elderly or sick relative.

Joe Lawrence born 1903

When I was still at school I used to work weekends as a lather boy in a barber's shop. I would go in about twelve o'clock and I would be working until eleven or twelve at night and on Sunday morning.... There were no safety razors in those days, all open cut, and men would have a shave about once a week for a penny and I would be lathering one face while he was shaving the other. If you didn't like him, you shoved soap in his mouth. Men didn't shave much at home in those days. I've known them come out of the Foundry Arms, have a shave and fall asleep in the chair, half loaded.

A mere thirty-one tribunal appeals were on grounds of conscience, most of them men opposed to war. These were either members of Colchester's small but vocal branch of the Independent Labour Party which was opposed to conscription, or nonconformist pacifists: one

Brethren, several Quakers and some members of Headgate Congregational Church, whose minister, Dr Dunkerley, was an active and outspoken conscientious objector. Indeed, although exempt from military service as an ordained minister, Dunkerley insisted on appearing before the tribunal himself, doubtless to proclaim his views and to support those from his church due to appear there too.

The Rev. Dr. Dunkerley of Headgate Chapel.

Conscientious objectors were usually questioned quite aggressively by Major Howard, told they were cowards or asked standard questions like what they would do faced with an armed German who assaulted their wife or daughter. Matters were saved by the presence on the tribunal of trade union representatives and the omnipresent Gurney Benham. In Colchester, at least, the tribunal system proved considered and civilised. In the street and in the town, however, even on the public platform, conscientious objectors were a constant butt of sarcasm and criticism. Though it might not be said openly, they were despised. Their courageous and principled views did not match the muscular Christianity of the Crusade against Evil, which the war had now become.

One solution to the shortage of men in the workforce was to employ women, and it is easy to rubbish contemporaries for not doing so more. But the cultural and practical problems were centuries old. Much male employment involved manual labour where strength was as significant as skill. A woman's commitment to her home, and the large families of 1914, was fundamental, and was that much greater if her husband was in France. When in 1915 it was proposed to establish a War Women's Service Committee, now that women could register their availability at Labour Exchanges, it took Pat Green, soon to become Colchester Council's second Labour Councillor, to point out that many women could at most only work half-time or part-time.

Nevertheless, younger Colchester women took on shopwork and worked long shifts in the factories. Land Army girls mastered farm work. Letters were delivered by a growing number of postwomen, while the town council gave licences to three women taxi drivers;

Ann Cudden, tram conductress, undergoing training. Mr Bullen, tramway manager, looks a bit upstaged.

employed fourteen much-photographed tram conductresses, and two female library assistants, busy, often without success, chasing up volumes which did not come back when their borrower went off to

Colchester's only ever female Town Sergeant with mayor Allen Aldridge.

France. Colchester's only ever female town sergeant looked after the mayor, still a man, and two borough policewomen were appointed, though it was not clear if they could arrest anyone.

All these were 'firsts' and quite revolutionary. Percy Sanders, who ran Paxman's, and was seconded to the town council in 1916, suggested they should employ women road workers. 'They do on the continent,' he pointed out. But nothing came of this, which, one suspects, might have been opposed by the fast-growing Workers Union whose local founder, Tim Smith, was currently the only Labour member of the town council. But if this proved a step too far, the co-option of Colchester's first two women councillors in 1918 was a major landmark, and, though it received far less attention at the time, so were Colchester's first two women doctors, both Indian, who were appointed to the Hospital following the loss of three male doctors to the Army.

War transformed the British economy, a war fuelled by mass production. From 1915 orders poured out of the new Ministry of Munitions: for shells, guns, uniforms, vehicles, equipment of all sorts.

Christmas Party 1916 at Crowther's Clothing factory. Mr Crowther stands at the back in their midst.

And the government always paid its bills – good news for manufacturers, even though it liquidated much of the nation's assets to do so. Suddenly, there was no unemployment, only a labour shortage. The gaps were filled by old men, boys under military age, and by women. In Colchester the workforce had never had it so good. The clothing and engineering factories worked long hours and pay was good. Shops also benefitted, not least from the spending power of the 20-30,000 soldiers in the town.

Colchester's seven specialist clothing factories, bearing the names of their founders, Hollington's, Hyam's, Leaning's, Crowther's, Hart & Levy's, Richmond & Lewis and the Colchester Manufacturing Company (called Turner's) made uniforms, while still, in most cases, turning out civilian overcoats and suits. Their women workers still recalled, seventy years later, the heavy rough serge of uniform material which could break an industrial sewing machine needle. By May 1915 the 350 women at the largest factory, Hollington's, a London-based firm, got through 12 tons of khaki a day, according to their manager, with an output of 500 overcoats, 500 tunics, 1,000 pairs of trousers and 7-800 riding breeches a week, a total of 20,000 military garments a month. To service this output the Great Eastern Railway would have had to deliver 72 tons of cut cloth to St Botolph's Station each week. It is easy to see why six of the seven clothing factories, all equally dependent on the delivery of cloth, were fairly close to this terminal. As capacity was enlarged, the level of war work in these factories was reflected in frequent newspaper advertisements for new 'hands'.

Such adverts also reflected the competition from the new jobs in munitions; for the greatest wartime innovation was the employment of women in engineering, an entirely male industry and an important one in Colchester. In August 1914 Paxman's, Colchester's largest company, employed just two women, doing tracings in the drawing office, in a workforce of over 800. By 1915, despite a belated government decision to prevent engineers enlisting, over 200 of those 800 men were in uniform; before long it was 300. As demand for shells in Flanders continued, the government decided to recruit women for the work. Colchester began later than many other engineering towns, as the relevant specialist machine tools took time to arrive at Paxman's, the designated centre. From December 1915 short training courses for munitions work, run mainly by Paxman staff, began at the Technical School on North Hill (today the Sixth Form College) for both men and women. By 1918 Paxman's workforce had reached 1,500, over 400 of whom were women.

Virtually all these women were employed in the mass production of a range of munitions: shells, mines and depth charges and their ancillary components. These were relatively simple items by Paxman standards but the key phrase is mass production, hitherto an alien concept to the firm. For over 40 years it had specialised in engine and boilers of ever-more sophisticated design. Planned in the drawing office, individual components were cast from molten metal in the foundry, then fine-tuned to thousandths of an inch by machine tools in the fitting shop. Engines (or boilers or compressors) were then assembled one at a time, not least because each one was likely to contain adaptions specific to its end purpose or destination, followed by rigorously testing prior to despatch. It was still largely true that a Paxman engine was only made when it had been ordered.

As a large engineering works, Paxman's would now have a very

Women assembling shells at Paxman's.

Paxman boiler works in full production.

busy war. As well as a night shift, and the late working of day shifts, working all Saturday and Sunday could also happen where orders were needed at short notice. Not only did Paxman's have to embrace mass production, but they continued to turn out their normal high tech products in some numbers, including nearly 300 large industrial boilers. There were also their ammonia and CO_2 compressors made for refrigerator units for the British arm of the German Linde Company. Since this was now an enemy company, a new company was floated, in which James Paxman took major shares, led by the British Linde managing director, Thomas Lightfoot, a close friend of James Paxman. This increased Paxman's output of refrigerator compressors for battleships, for chemical works, for most UK explosive factories and for new margarine factories fostered by the UK government to supply a vital alternative to butter. Paxman's also took on the manufacture of 4,600 ice moulds, items hitherto supplied by the Linde Company from Germany.

The Paxman Board in 1916. Seated (left to right) Captain William Paxman, James Paxman, Wilson Marriage, Percy Sanders.

The key figure at Paxman's was Percy Sanders, its managing director. Initially he enlisted for military service, passed through three regiments before being sent back to Colchester to run his company, now under Admiralty control. Competent, hard-working and young, he worked all hours, sometimes not going home at night, cat-napping in his office during the night shift, which the firm ran throughout the war. He also won his spurs with his large workforce, some of whom later recalled him working all night, with his coat off, with a 14-inch file to finish an urgent order for a new type of naval mine.

When in 1915 David Lloyd George became Minister of Munitions and instigated a drive to increase the output of munitions, Sanders' role became regionally pivotal. Lloyd George famously recruited industrialists to 'run the war'. As President of the East Anglian Engineering Employers Federation Percy Sanders held face to face talks with the future Prime Minister and put together what became The East Anglian Munitions Committee, heads of regional engineering firms undertaking a shared programme of munitions production. In so doing Paxman's came under the Treasury Agreement, hammered out by Lloyd George with the trade unions whereby they accepted 'dilution', the use of unskilled or semi-skilled workers to do work traditionally reserved for fully-apprenticed 'skilled' workers, with the undertaking to involve unions in the war work and restore the status quo after the war. In this way Paxman's secured four years of industrial peace, unlike some other areas of Britain. For the first time the firm built and operated a works canteen, offsetting its cost against its excess profits tax.

His regional role strengthened Sanders' hand in a long-running struggle with government agencies, which sought to divert some of Paxman's most experienced men to exercise their skills in the armed forces, in spite of their protected status. Sanders felt strong enough to take this up directly with Lloyd George and the evidence is that it produced rapid results. Reviewing the firm's achievements at the end of hostilities, Percy Sanders, not one for exaggeration, claimed that:

> *'with the possible exemption of a few armaments firms, no firm undertook and carried out such a variety of complicated and accurate work so successfully and in such large numbers as Davey, Paxman & Co.'*

A marine gun manufactured by Paxman for the navy.

This involved, he calculated, tens of millions of precision-machined components. Specifically, they made 250,000 shells of several types, 70,000 adapters and fuse plugs for these, 20,000 depth charges, 4,000 mines, 80,000 mine extras of various kinds, eighty various types of guns, 7,600 extractor gears and 500 hulls for tanks. There were thousands of component parts for tractors and lorries, and an entire plant was installed for making aeroplane parts, all items for which the firm had no prior experience.

Much thought was put into streamlining and simplifying the manufacture of these components. For this the firm received praise and more orders. Not all were simple. An order for 180 Sandford generators for use in submarines, a new product to Paxman's, involved the production and assembly of 1,700 named parts for each one. Complete engines and boilers for 'Standard' ships and East Coast drifters were equally novel. All this new work required specialist machine tools, new workshops, and the conversion of storage areas into further workshops. Space was so tight that the women machining shell cases worked in the gangways of an existing workshop, literally back to back, kitted up in blue overalls and tight mop hats to keep long hair out of fast moving machinery.

Technically all these women were unskilled, not having gone through a traditional apprenticeship training, but in practice they learnt quickly. Their supervisors were recruited from the best families and included the daughters of Captain (now Major) Paxman and Mrs Slaughter. Like the men, the women handled dangerous machinery. Annie Stevens, who helped train recruits, lost part of a finger in a lathe.

Paxman munition workers in their standard uniform.

'I have never seen anyone so brave and plucky in my life', wrote Miss Paxman to Annie Stevens's mother. 'We were happy working together for our country', was Annie's comment seventy years later.

WORKING IN MUNITIONS

Gladys Hayhoe, born 1901
He asked me how old I was. I said, 'I shall be 16 next month'. He said, 'Start tomorrow'.... We went into the turnery [at Paxman's]. Just inside the door was small guns being made and we turned right and I had to pass a gun barrel that was being made. It was on a lathe that went by itself... [and] the barrel was as long as this house!

Olive Manning, born 1889
The boy I was going out with went to the war and [in] about a month he was killed, and so I left and went to work at munitions. Twelve hours a day: 6 in the morning to 6 at night, and 6 at night the next week till 6 in the morning. Very hard work. Big shells like that [puts arms apart], naval shells. At the Britannia. An old

---

fashioned lathe – German! ....There were four operations. They put on a copper band. First of all I had to cut it, let the chuck drive - out front. And I put another two on. They go like that, up and down [does gesture]*, and I had to push a gasket screw in and then connect the top...They were very heavy shells. Work was very, very hard.... Oh – and when they painted them the smell was dreadful!*

The women were paid a flat rate for their 12-hour day – or night – shift as the case may be. A weekly wage of up to £1 was a handsome sum for a teenage girl, when boy apprentices of the same age might only receive ten shillings (50p) a week, since Percy Sanders paid women the same rate as men for the same work. Like the girls and women in the clothing factories there was a camaraderie among them, even that sense of a noble cause which we saw in the War Work Depot. As the war ground on, despite high wages, new staff became harder and harder to find. Such was the shortage of skilled men that those same boy apprentices might, before they were 18, take on supervisory jobs or the work of skilled men. Many girls were employed while still 15, pending

Paravanes under manufacture at Paxman's.

their sixteenth birthday. Some travelled long distances to work from other parts of the county such as Brightlingsea, Clacton and even Halstead.

As noted in Chapter 2 Paxman's was one of only three British firms to be chosen for secret Admiralty work. This involved the manufacture of 1,100 paravanes, code named 'otters', twin floats which dragged a hawser across the cables which held German mines just below the surface, sliding it along to a cutting tool. The mine then floated and could be detonated by gunfire. Paxman's also made the derricks, which raised and lowered the 'otters' into the water, Percy Sanders contributing to its design. After trial and error in their use, strung between two ships steaming side by side, 'otters' proved 100 per cent successful.

Given the range of orders the firm handled, staff at Paxman were well used to government representatives touring the works. More surprising was the arrival at a day's notice of a delegation from the Russian Duma or Parliament, our eastern allies, in May 1916, who were here in connection with a package to keep a faltering Russian Army equipped. It was led by no less a figure than Alexander Protopopov, Vice-President of the Duma, and General Gourko, a future Chief of the Imperial General Staff. Travelling from London by road, they arrived at Marks Tey Station where a group of schoolchildren sang the Russian National Anthem – a remarkable achievement at a day's notice.

The special launch equipment for paravanes was pioneered by Paxman's (Paxman Archive Trust).

Postcard recording the visit of the Russian delegation to Colchester in 1916.

Paxman's, which had exported its portable engines to both Russia and Germany before the war, had been chosen to produce munitions, portable engines and boilers specific to Russia's needs. The visit sparked a good deal of civic excitement. Speeches, a parade of Town Councillors and a display by troops on the Abbey Field, preceded a tour of Colchester castle and lunch at the town hall. Finally, they got to visit the Paxman Works on Hythe Hill. Whether their orders ever arrived is unclear, given the effective collapse of the Russian war effort just over a year later. Protopopov was briefly proclaimed 'dictator' in February 1917, before being executed by the Bolsheviks.

Such a detailed look at one Colchester factory reminds us that there were during the war several Colchester communities. Paxman's and Hollington's, whose workforces spent more time together than they did with their own families, were each in their way a distinct world. Amid noisy, repetitive work affectionate nicknames abounded, and black

humour often enlivened their well-paid, four year's hard work. In the
Munition Workers' Football League they encountered fellow workers
from Colchester's other engineering works. There was even a Munition
Workers' Sports Day, twice won by Mumford's, second in size after
Paxman's.

With their workforce of 400, Mumford's were specialist marine
engineers. They too came under Admiralty control and as such could
not accept contracts for munitions. Instead they provided their products
for warships: 2,500 patent feed water regulators for the large boilers
in warships, nearly 3,000 pumps of all sizes, high speed engines and
boilers for numbers of picket boats, fourteen sets of their triple-
expansion engines for minesweepers, an engine of their own design
for the kite balloons used to detect submarines and some 100 sets of
marine motors for small boats. Like Paxman's they also undertook
production of small components and an amount of marine repair work
in Harwich harbour.

The Britannia Works, closed in 1914, came back from the dead to
make munitions. The Colchester Lathe Company, with a workforce of
more than eighty, continued to make centre lathes, but were kept busy
making shells in some numbers, as were Bracketts, who also made their
specialist pumps and filters. Both these firms were at the Hythe, as
were Woods who made small electric motors and industrial fans. Here

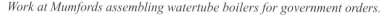

Work at Mumfords assembling watertube boilers for government orders.

One of the Rennie Forrest trawlers used for mine sweeping during the War. (Nottage Institute)

too was the Paisley Engineering Company, which made engines so badly that they actually managed to go bust in wartime. Work sub-contracted to them by Paxman's was a nightmare to put right.

Sub-contracting by the large factories nonetheless offered opportunity. Mr Stone, erstwhile garage owner of St Botolph's Street, diversified into small calibre shells, transforming his fortunes with an enlarged workforce of twelve. Indeed, no venture was too small, no corner too remote for military orders to be placed. Working out of the Hythe, Frank Wright, haulage contractor, with his solid tyre motor lorries, was rushed off his feet by the military. Over on Mersea, excluded from much of their traditional fishing grounds, Herbert Welham, manager of Gowan's the sail-makers, had fifty hands, most of them women, cutting and sewing canvas pillow cases, canvas buckets, canvas stretchers and canvas kit bags. Within a year this operation employed 450, while Mr Littlehale's smithy turned out a thousand mule shoes for the many donkeys requisitioned by the Army.

The bridge from Wivenhoe to Rowhedge under construction by the Royal Engineers.

Rather more substantial were the 215-ton trawlers built at the Rennie Forrests' Shipyard at Wivenhoe. Used as mine sweepers during the war, they returned to fishing afterwards. Here too some women were employed. Here too the constant stream of troops and equipment provided an unlooked-for bonus. It had often been suggested that a bridge from Wivenhoe to Rowhedge on the opposite bank, where the Rowhedge Ironworks employed so many men, was desirable. Now the Royal Engineers built one, making the little ferry quite superfluous. It was 'opened' in person by the King in July 1916. Disliked by the sailing barges, which plied the seas route to London, the bridge was dismantled after the war.

And if pay was good in the shipyards, workshops and factories, profits were better. Local firms which had been struggling found new life. Paxman's, who had even registered losses in the pre-war years, turned in the best profits of their fifty-year history between 1915 and 1919, enabling James Paxman, the main shareholder, now over 80, to live in some style at Bournemouth.

All over Colchester people were working long hours. And if anyone was still without a job, '100 men wanted at once for New Explosives Company at Stowmarket' was a typical 1915 advertisement in the

Colchester press. Several town councillors, prominent members of the business community, resigned from the council because of pressure of work, something hitherto unknown. Their replacements were all co-opted; this was no time for elections. Similarly, as the war ground on, the Oyster Feast, the Thieves' Dinner, the Mayor's Ball and other landmarks in Colchester's social calendar were suspended for the duration, though the town council still found time to robe up and proclaim the centuries-old St Dennis Fair from the town hall steps, while the Essex Archaeological Society were slow to cancel their summer programme of excursions. Tradition was almost sacred in Colchester, and everyday life continued; but 'business as usual' this was not.

CHAPTER 7

Food for All

At 7.30 am one morning in January 1918, while it was still dark, the mayor of Colchester, Councillor Jarmin, in his role as Chairman of the Food Control Committee, made his way with two of his committee to Long Wyre Street where he was confronted by a crowd of 2,000 people. That is a lot of people for Long Wyre Street at 7.30 am, but they all were waiting at the Maypole Dairy for its twice weekly delivery of margarine which was now the only source of margarine in Colchester. What they did not know was why the mayor was there.

Since butter was now almost unobtainable, margarine was essential for that English staple, bread and butter, though not, happily, for another staple, bread and dripping – animal fats, usually beef, were kept carefully in an old pot in most kitchens. The 2,000 were not really hungry, let alone starving, but like others up and down the country, very grumpy. The government, however, concerned at growing national unrest about food shortages, feared there would be food riots. This was conveyed to Jarmin in confidential government briefings, along with a date at which a measure would empower chairmen of Food Control Committees to commandeer food supplies where it was 'in the public interest'. Jarmin resolved to be proactive on the day this measure became law.

The bi-weekly crowds in Wyre Street had been gathering for some time and Jarmin's committee felt sure they would be acting in the public interest. Prepared if necessary to read the Riot Act, Jarmin, in his own words,

By 1918 queues outside Colchester shops were not like this, carefully staged for the camera with the help of TWO policemen. Note the number of children queuing.

> *...mounted the* [delivery] *van and formally commandeered half the consignment, consisting of two tons of margarine. A large board and a piece of chalk* [announced] *that margarine would be on sale in an hour in 12 different centres in Colchester at the fixed controlled price. The crowd applauded and trouble was at an end for that day.*

Later the mayor could be seen outside the town hall selling wrapped slabs of margarine at fixed prices to women shoppers. Such commandeering continued daily until formal rationing was introduced. Indeed, similar measures were being adopted all over Essex.

As the war wore on food shortages had troubled all the combatants. Colchester's margarine crisis hardly matched the starving crowds in Germany and Turkey. That Britain, which imported over half its food in 1914, avoided such scenes reflects the strength of its economic and social structure, but in Colchester, as in the wider country, it was only achieved by belated change and anxious intervention by the borough

Let them eat cake. The 'largest cake ever made in Forest Gate', sent to members of the Ammunition column of the East Anglian Brigade, met by a delegation at Colchester's North Station.

council. Colchester's lot was all the harder from simultaneously having to meet the food needs of so many troops in training.

As we saw in Chapter 2, from the outset of war, the government had moved to secure vital supplies like Canadian wheat and the sugar so central to the viability of Tiptree's jam factory. Most sugar however was imported, so UK sugar beet production was rapidly expanded and imports of cane sugar from the West Indies renegotiated. Such measures settled any initial run on food, but the government was equally swift to urge the civilian population to avoid waste and eschew hoarding, a message which was spread across Colchester by government posters. Initially however little was done to put farming on a war footing, as was clear in Colchester's agricultural hinterland.

Here farmers still resented the seizure of their draft horses in 1914 and, increasingly, the loss of so many young labourers to the armed forces as they continued to operate the farms in their traditional way. This meant mixed livestock and grain production remained the local pattern. Since government continued to import grain and meat in large quantities from North America, the harvest of 1915 proved adequate, helped in the Colchester district by soldiers from the garrison and young boys still of school age. Indeed, the local wheat acreage was the largest it had been for many years. There seemed no need to question whether, for example, Colchester's two large rose-growing businesses, both run by members of the Cant family, should be devoting both fields and manpower to growing roses, and touring Britain all summer competing for trophies.

Benjamin Cant, Colchester's leading rose grower, sits with his staff before an impressive set of national silverware.

This approach to food supply was increasingly risky as Germany's sophisticated U-boats became capable of sinking British merchant ships bringing supplies across the Atlantic, and sinking them faster than the shipyards could replace them. From 1916 the government belatedly began to organise food production. In May they introduced British Standard Time, hoping to benefit farming and maintain coal stocks by advancing clocks one hour to take advantage of the extra daylight of the summer months.

The move was rather celebrated in Colchester since the man who had led the campaign for this, William Willett, was the son of a Colchester native whose family still lived in the town. The national spotlight led Alderman Watts, a stonemason by trade, to promise to put up a statue in Willett's honour. Hard times and Watts's death in 1918 reduced this to a bronze bust, which subsequently sat, rather lost, in

Major Hetherington, third from left, with the prototype tank.

the museum collection long after Willett had been forgotten. Oddly, the town showed no comparable enthusiasm for an actual resident, Major Hetherington of Berechurch Hall, a key player in the invention of the tank, whose initial design had now been taken up by Churchill.

Meanwhile the response of Colchester farmers to daylight saving was to behave as if it had not happened. At a meeting called by Wilson Marriage, they decided to 'work by the sun' and ignore the changes in the clock. A more positive initiative came in April when Marriage arranged a demonstration of a Mogul oil (i.e. petrol) tractor in a field off Harwich Road belonging to Dilbridge Hall where Marriage himself farmed. It is received wisdom that the First World War led to increased agricultural mechanisation. This seems to have been minimal in North East Essex until the last months of the war. So late as autumn 1917 there were still only twenty-seven tractors in use on Essex farms, compared with 811 steam portable engines and 292 steam traction engines. In February 1918, large numbers attended Layer Road Football ground to be shown the Eros tractor attachment, a Heath-Robinson device which could be attached to the back of a Ford Model

T car. Given the clay soils of Essex this was hardly an answer to the county's needs.

Then there was the county's War Agricultural Committee (WAC) set up by the government in the autumn of 1915. Chaired by Edward Strutt, the county's leading milk producer, it had representatives from every part of Essex, who in turn set up local committees. Francis Dent, a civil servant, maintained the link with the Ministry of Agriculture. With the entire county to concern it, the committee's initial impact on North East Essex was minimal. This was perhaps just as well. The government's drive to plough up grass to increase crop acreage was thought too simple by half, given the continued need to provide cows

Tractors: by 1918 adverts like this began appearing in the Colchester press.

with grazing. Moreover, ploughed grassland rarely produced good crops: it took several years to eliminate pests like wireworm and leather jackets.

The local harvest of 1916, which once more depended on the temporary labour of schoolchildren and soldiers, was particularly poor, and the increased wheat acreage of 1915 was not equalled. This had nothing to do with bad management, but much to do with local crop rotations. In dry north Essex it was still unwise to grow wheat in a field two years running, notwithstanding a government offer of a guaranteed price. In practice local farming decisions followed custom, but as market prices for both grain and meat rose markedly, farmers actually began to have a profitable war.

The American harvest of 1916 was also bad, and this, plus increasing U-Boat successes, led to a Ministry of Food being set up to regulate food supply against the increasingly obvious shortages in the shops. Matters came to a head in February 1917 when Germany, in a desperate gamble to end the war, introduced unrestricted submarine warfare, sinking any shipping heading for Britain. This was spectacularly successful, reducing Britain to six-week's supply of wheat and was only countered when the Admiralty and the new Prime

Soldiers helping to weed the soft fruit fields at Tiptree Farm (The John Wilkin Collection).

Minister, Lloyd George, belatedly adopted the use of Atlantic convoys. This in turn made possible the destruction of an increasing number of U-boats.

Meanwhile the landmark Corn Production Act guaranteed minimum prices for wheat (to make bread) and oats (to feed horses), specified a minimum wage for agricultural workers of twenty-five shillings a week, and established the Agricultural Wages Board to replace the open warfare between farmers and agricultural trade unions which had been a feature of North Essex for twenty years. This move did not please local farmers. They were even less pleased in 1918 when the board awarded farm workers a rise to thirty-two shillings a week in recognition of continued wartime inflation. Meeting in Colchester's Corn Exchange the local branch of the National Farmers' Union voted their unanimous opposition.

A new Minister of Food Control, Lord Rhondda, now introduced compulsion, and the Essex WAC went in search of grassland to plough up. Local objections abounded, but the end result was an increase in arable acreage of 1,000 acres in Lexden & Winstree and 600 in Tendring, hardly a revolution, and well below the target figure. Dogged foot dragging saw many a farmer through to the Armistice and only a few like Benjamin Clarke of Rye House Farm at Layer-de-la-Haye finished up in court, fined £25 for not ploughing up his grass. Today that field is still there, overlooking Abberton Reservoir. Farmers were equally unhappy when their free-market profits were curbed. Maximum prices set for milk, for meat and for wheat represented a government takeover of farming.

At the same time the demands of conscription, now impacting on older married men, brought strident protest from local farmers as farm workers previously exempted were called up. In this the farmers got the full support of the WAC, and the problem remained till the end of the war, a bad example of un-joined-up government. The harvests of 1917 and 1918 therefore required the same major deployment of home troops and the widespread employment of schoolboys, permitted by Essex Education Committee to work on farms for six weeks between May and the end of July for a maximum eight hours a day and a minimum wage of three shillings and sixpence a week. The need was real. To take one example, the large Armoury Farm at West Bergholt, home of the brewery family Daniells, was now reduced to a workforce of eight men aged 50 to 79, plus a 16-year-old boy. However now help came in two other forms: German prisoners of war and women.

By the harvest of 1917 over 800 German prisoners of war were working on Essex farms, paid five shillings a week for a nine-hour day. With many held on Mersea Island, they worked on farms there and in small numbers across North East Essex. In 1918 a large block advert in the local press encouraged farmers to apply for them for use in harvest work. In Colchester some were housed in the cricket pavilion in Castle Park whence they were engaged in cleaning out the river.

The employment of women in agriculture was hardly new. Women had long undertaken seasonal part-time work and Essex was a county with an important milk industry. But this was about women replacing the missing men. A survey conducted in eleven of the fourteen Essex districts in 1916 found 24 per cent of the pre-war agricultural labour force had joined the armed forces. This would rise to 35 per cent once conscription began. In February 1916 the Essex Women's War Agricultural Association, chaired by Lady Petre, the war widow of a leading Essex landowner, launched a voluntary scheme. A female registrar was to be appointed in every village to compile a list of women willing to work in agriculture. The Colchester registrar, Pat Green, soon to be co-opted as a borough councillor, launched her initiative in May, but it is not clear what it achieved.

In March 1917 came the formation of the Women's Land Army.

Women weeding fields at Thorpe.

The 'Lady Carter', a land army girl working at Tiptree Fruit Farm (The John Wilkin Collection).

This too struggled in Essex and was described as 'liable to leakages'. After the briefest of training, young women were often sent to 'remote outposts' where loneliness led them to quit. Though by September there were now '7,000 women on the land' in Essex, over half of these were part-time and only 120 appear to have been full-time Land Army recruits, paid, trained, and equipped with official uniforms. Around Colchester five trained at Peldon; others at Layer-de-la-Haye; some at Tiptree Fruit Farm and at least one at Boxted, where Annie Russell learnt to plough 'as well as any man, with a team of two heavy horses.'

Perhaps for this reason Colchester was chosen to launch a Land Army recruitment drive in June 1918. It took the form of a massive procession, led by a military brass band, fifty boy scouts, Scottish pipers and a long line of twelve wagons carrying animals and vegetables of every kind, Land Army women in uniforms, marching, carrying inspirational banners, holding or wielding all sorts of agricultural equipment, kindly supplied for the day by Joslins, Colchester's leading agricultural retailers. The route chosen for this procession is instructive. It began at the Hythe and wound its way up

Hythe Hill and Magdalen Street to St Botolph's Corner and then up Queen Street to Castle Park. In this way it travelled through the heart of the largest working class district of Colchester. The sub-text was clear: patriotism was one thing; a second household income was another. A rally in Castle Park, addressed by the mayor, concluded with an inspirational speech by the Honourable Mrs Lyttelton from the Ministry of Agriculture. By 1919 there were over 500 Land Army women in Essex.

These rather laboured efforts to mobilise agricultural output in North East Essex are in contrast to the robust self-help of Colchester's Land Cultivation Committee (LCC) and its ruthless pursuit of land fit for allotments. In 1914 Colchester already had some 134 acres of allotments and over 1,000 allotment holders. Growing your own vegetables was embedded in the community. Flower, fruit and vegetable shows, complete with multiple prizes, abounded, indeed were an important part of Colchester's cultural heritage, where a market garden industry had (pardon the pun) deep roots. The leader in this field was the Colchester Rose and Horticultural Society. Early in 1915 it began to urge the need for a systematic growing of vegetables on Colchester allotments and organised lectures on the subject. In 1916, as shortages began to seriously irk shoppers, the government empowered local authorities to take over 'unoccupied land' for allotments. Thus was formed the LCC.

Like adventurers exploring a new continent they scoured the borough for vacant sites. Colchester was still a town surrounded by and interspersed with open spaces and the LCC was not disappointed. Indeed they were even approached by owners of patches who sensed a business opportunity: would the borough be interested in their land at a rent of £100? Politely the Committee said no, unless it was made available *pro bono*. The sheer number of new allotment sites established, many quite small, is impressive, too many to list in full, but Castle Park, the Grammar School playing fields, land behind the Military Hospital, behind the gas works, at East Bay, at Mile End, at Lexden, off Hythe Hill, up Harwich Road; land owned by developers but not yet developed, all yielded their spaces.

Nor was there a lack of takers, all strictly catechised about their new responsibilities, of fighting the war on the garden front. Seeds were secured at cost from seed merchants and manure from the garrison at

Colchester allotments established in 1917 are still in use today.

a 'nominal price'. Two consignments of seed potatoes, 12 and 20 tons respectively, secured by the Essex War Agricultural Committee from Scotland, were carefully dispensed. By the end of the war Colchester had consolidated 227 acres of allotments (that's 130 football pitches), tended by 2,200 plot holders, thus serving more than one in five of Colchester households. A spokesman for the Ministry for National Service announced that for a town of its size, it was 'streets ahead of any in England and Wales'. Nor should we forget that most Colchester houses had gardens, where vegetables might be grown or chickens kept. To these in 1917 the LCC distributed 20,000 free cabbage plants and 100 breeding fowls. Air-tight jars for preserving fruit were bought in bulk and sold at cost to householders. All this helped cushion the growing frustration with shortages in the shops.

It was not just shortages; it was also rising prices. A Colchester working class family spent about one fifth of its total food budget on bread or flour. In 1914 a standard 4lb loaf had cost 6d. By Christmas 1916 it cost 10d; by January 1918 one shilling. Sugar prices rose even faster. The cheaper cuts of meat, such as working families might eat, almost doubled in price, so increasingly they ate bacon instead. Fortunately, full employment enabled most to absorb the cost, particularly as some wage gains described as 'war bonuses' were made, though middle class households on fixed incomes were less fortunate.

The Royal Eastern Counties Institution with its large staff and hundreds of resident special needs patients navigated the war with great difficulty. Despite having its own farm, food shortages in 1917-18 proved a nightmare.

Charitable bodies like the Hospital and the Royal Eastern Counties Institution for those with mental disability, both dependent for income on voluntary donations, suffered particularly from inflation.

But it was shortages that angered the public the most. As 1917 wore on and the U-Boat campaign intensified, 'sold out' became a familiar notice in shop windows before midday. From having to shop early it was a small step to queuing before a shop opened. All this took time, as word of mouth tip-offs became a good housewife's guide. So did positioning your children in several queues, even putting two children in one queue, thereby gaining a double ration. Goodwill suffered. Shopkeepers was widely accused of favouring certain customers over others. Understandably they valued long-serving customers and the spending power of the more affluent, but were also seeking to be even-handed. The foundrymen at Paxman's threatened to strike if their wives had to go on queuing so long. An unexpected delivery of cheese to a grocers in Crouch Street led to a raid on the van by women shoppers – the only case of this to occur in Colchester.

QUEUING FOR FOOD

Ella Caney, born 1897
You was always out shopping trying to get something to eat. There was no rationing then – you got what you could. You went down town every morning and you'd hear the rumour that there was something at one shop and something at another and you'd stand in a queue.

Fred Ridgley, born 1901
There were six in our family and sometimes all us children were standing in different queues.

The government's initial response was to urge restraint. From February 1917 all citizens were asked to restrict themselves to 4lbs of bread, 2½lbs of meat and ¾lb sugar a week. Next came the suggestion to have two 'meatless days' and two 'potato-less days' a week. This proposal gained a vague endorsement from King George V, which was rapidly re-spun as 'the King's Pledge'. Great efforts were made in Colchester to get citizens to 'take the King's Pledge'. It was even sent round to all schools and 14 June was set aside as King's Pledge Day for all those over 16. According to the mayor, Councillor Jarmin, 'Practically all responsible citizens signed and forwarded to the mayor's parlour the King's Pledge… and displayed in the house window a card with purple ribbon notifying that all within were "in honour bound to observe the King's Pledge".' It seems very likely that this was more universal in the middle class world which Jarmin inhabited than the more deprived districts of Colchester. In December a personal letter from the mayor on 'food economy' was delivered by boy scouts to all 10,000 Colchester households, while leading Nonconformist ministers urged prohibition on the sale of alcohol.

In point of fact alcohol had been under attack for some time, under the cold stare of DORA. The King made it known he would abstain until the war was over. The Bishop of Chelmsford had urged all Colchester Christians to abstain. Opening hours had been reduced, beer officially weakened, heavy taxation had doubled its price; and all spirits, sold only in large bottles to inhibit sales, were reduced to 70

The local Band of Hope make children the shock troops of the Temperance campaign, as their procession heads up St John's Street.

Under attack from the strong Temperance lobby in Colchester, the town's leading brewery, Daniell's, placed this advert in the local papers proclaiming the merits of beer as a temperance drink.

BEER AS A TEMPERANCE DRINK.

is a remarkable fact that, at a time when domestic controversies have ceased in face of the great peril, the teetotal campaign should have been renewed with or than ever before.

is the old indiscriminate campaign against any beverage which contains an appreciable amount of alcohol, regardless of its dilution, or of any other elements uish one kind of alcoholised beverage from another kind. This also is a remarkable fact, for it shows at once the unreasonable character of the agitation. e suppression of vodka in Russia and of absinthe in France are quoted as parallel cases with the proposed suppression of all kinds of fermented and dis ges in Britain. This discloses a most unwarrantable confusion of thought. It shows a misconception of the word temperance.

dka, is a fiery spirit, drunk neat, and so often drunk to excess. Absinthe is a deleterious compound. With all forms of spirit drinking there is a danger of g moderation unless the drinker keeps a guard over his potations

t such criticisms do not apply to ale and the other fermented liquors of low alcoholic strength. They are mild and wholesome, and a person must drink the ous excess before he can become intoxicated by them.

the **CHANCELLOR OF THE EXCHEQUER** says, **BEER IN ALCOHOLIC STRENGTH** is "**JUST A LITTLE ABOVE GINGER A** ghout the world, and throughout the history of the world, mankind has demanded some stimulant property in its liquid food—even the tea drinker wants it is natural and innocent. It is not to be crushed as essentially evil, but rather to be guided in such a manner as will eliminate the chances of abuse. should, therefore, encourage the use of a beverage which, while providing the desired stimulant, will provide it in such a diluted form as will remove the d a beverage which will at the same time be palatable and contain healthful properties. **ALE AND STOUT FULFIL THESE CONDITIONS.** BEER," an eminent authority has declared, "**IS THE ONLY SAFE DRINK.**" It is the national beverage of Englishmen. **IT IS PURE;** for the mat nutafacture and the conditions under which it is manufactured give it beyond doubt a **PURITY WHICH NO OTHER BEVERAGE CAN CLAIM** ts nourishment—it facilitates the digestion of other nutriment; it has tonic properties. The alcohol in modern beer is present in only just sufficient quantity to e ul, as an alcoholic beverage at all

Beer, therefore, is pre-eminently the Temperance Drink.

tent of drunkenness in the country at the present time is greatly exaggerated, and investigation of such drunkenness as there is would show that only a negligible part of it was due to the drinking of beer. er a smaller view, worth remembering that the Chancellor of the Exchequer has raised moderate beer duties to a patriotic height. Mr. **Lloyd George** (making good his words) says, " EVERY HALF-PINT THAT A HE WILL BE CONTRIBUTING TO THE CARRYING ON OF THE WAR."

ELL & SONS' BREWERIES, LTD., WEST BERGHOLT AND COLCHESTER, have long held a high reputation for **WHOLESOME, PURE, & PALATABLE BEERS & STOL** PRICES and copy of LEAFLET will be sent post free on application to the Brewery, West Bergholt; or to the Castle Brewery, Maidenburgh Street, Colchester.

per cent proof (that's 40 per cent proof today). Officially it was illegal to 'treat' another man to a drink. Daniells, the large brewers at West Bergholt, felt the need to take a half-page advert in the paper to defend the continued brewing of beer. In 1917 DORA restricted beer output to 70 per cent of that for 1916. By 1918 beer was in such short supply that pubs might only open certain days of the week. In Colchester, as in the nation, weekend drunkenness greatly reduced, a state that continued after the war.

And not only beer was in trouble. The contents of bread was progressively altered. The milling process was changed; grains other than wheat were added, making the standard loaf what we would call wholemeal and contemporaries, raised on the virtue of all-white bread, would call, rather ungenerously, black bread. It was unpalatable, even if the authorities said it was more nutritious. By 1918 potato flour was also being added, so that there was, it was claimed, only one baker left in Colchester who did not add it to his loaves. In 1916 potatoes, themselves a staple of English diet, had been in trouble too. There was a poor domestic harvest and shortages became common. Limited price controls were imposed. Queuing for potatoes became a Colchester cliché, so that in 1917 vigorous efforts were made by the Army to grow them in bulk at Middlewick, and few allotments holders neglected to raise them.

Beyond food, there was a serious shortage of paper. The local newspapers all shrank in size and advertised their wish to buy used paper. More seriously, throughout the war there were regular concerns in Colchester about coal supplies. Not only was coal extensively used for domestic heating but Colchester's factories needed it too. With so many miners volunteering for Kitchener's Army, coal output became a national concern, and with the army dominating so much rail usage and the traditional alternative of sea transport disrupted by war, delivery became erratic. Local engineering firms who made their own advance orders could not be sure they would arrive. By March 1915 the largest domestic supplier, the Colchester Co-op, felt the need to restrict its loyal customers to one and a half hundredweight (76kg) a week.

In November, following a similar scheme in London, Colchester Town Council held a four-hour Coal Conference with all the local suppliers. Here it was agreed to fix prices at eight to ten shillings per ton, depending on quality, charging one shilling above London prices

Queuing for potatoes became universal in 1917. Macklin's at St Botolph's Corner was a major supplier. Note the boy with the black arm band, evidence of a death in the family.

to cover the higher freight costs. By the summer of 1917 matters were bad again, and continued so for the rest of the war. On one occasion coal already loaded in trucks for Colchester was rushed in emergency to France. Recognising that most of the poor did not have coal storage facilities and could not therefore buy their winter supply in advance, the Council nagged the Board of Trade's Coal Controller to release 1,000 tons to be stored at Colchester for sale to small purchasers that winter. They finally got 750 tons in two instalments.

As food concerns rose throughout 1917, children were taken out of school to become hunter-gatherers. In 1917 they were supervised to pick 220 tons of blackberries, much of which found its way to the Tiptree jam factory. Next, 8 tons of horse chestnuts were harvested; their skins could provide the acetone needed for the explosive content of shells. Finally, children were mobilised for murder, as the WAC declared war on pests. Across the Tendring peninsular 53,644 rats were killed over 1917-18. By using strychnine they also took out cats. At Wivenhoe children were paid 2d for every rat's tail; at Rowhedge it was 1d. Lexden & Winstree paid out 3d for every twelve sparrow heads. Thousands died. In 1918 some 81,000 caterpillars were snatched before any surviving sparrows might eat them, while Colchester, anxious to defend its free cabbages, financed the killing of 80,000 cabbage white butterflies. Young Alfred Scrutton of Old Heath personally did for 1,500. And out on the river estuary where the oyster fishery was doing rather well, 150 tons of slipper limpets, an invasive American sea snail, were dredged off the bottom each week to be sold as fertiliser at 10s a ton.

As 1917 ended the margarine crowds in Wyre Street were matched by angry scenes outside other shops with queues. Government posters urging citizens to avoid food waste at Christmas were seen everywhere, but the mayor's fund could still support a Christmas Dinner for 800 wounded patients at the Military Hospital, part of the 3,000 sick and wounded currently being cared for in Colchester. Hospitals also made heavy demands on limited local milk supplies. Early in January the sinking of several ships carrying imported meat left most Colchester butchers with nothing to sell. Some shut up shop. Up at the Eastern Counties Institution with its 250 patients, its medical director, Dr. Turner, found his own meat by buying a couple of bullocks and a few

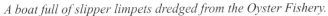

A boat full of slipper limpets dredged from the Oyster Fishery.

sheep. Oral testimony implies there was a local black market in pork and lots of poached rabbits. One interviewee recalls collecting an armchair at the railway goods station stuffed full of food.

Amid this crisis a meeting was held at the Co-op Hall where earlier that month an indignant working class group had broken with tradition and voted to support a candidate at the anticipated General Election. Also present were the leaders of the local Labour Party, anchored on the trade union presence in the town. The war years and the full employment of its factories had been central to the establishment of an assertive labour movement in Colchester. Complaints were made that 'food distribution was not being properly controlled' and shopkeepers who took advantage of the situation were attacked. A resolution 'to abolish profiteering and introduce equal rationing for rich and poor' was passed unanimously. 'Let them treat the duke and the dustman alike', was a popular cry.

The mayor was now formally approached by a delegation led by the formidable Councillor Tim Smith, founder of the local branch of the Workers Union. Representing, he pointed out, 'over 3,000 members' he demanded that this labour should have equal representation on the Food Control Committee and that women workers in laundries and munitions should be represented too. The mayor was quite brisk. Their delegation, he declared, only represented

The military made added demand on food supplies: the dining room at the Military Hospital, with men dressed in their 'hospital blues'.

a minority; there would be no change. A frosty relationship between labour and the council lay ahead. In fact the meeting had already been overtaken by events.

Lord Rhondda had decided that government-controlled rationing and government control over food distribution must happen. This was to be organised by the Food Control Committees, operating under a welter of food-related Orders, introduced under DORA's umbrella. Since, legally, citizens needed to be informed of each order, the local press found its front pages filled with bizarre injunctions; one example will suffice:

THE BRITISH ONIONS ORDER 1917
For the attention of dealers in and growers of British Onions.

1. No person except a regular wholesale or retail dealer purchasing for resale shall in any week directly or indirectly purchase a greater quantity of British onions than 7lbs in all.
2. No person shall sell British onions by retail unless he is a person registered under the Potato Order 1917....

[And so on, for 8 clauses]

As the tentacles of control grew, so did the orders. By November 1918 Colchester's Food Control Committee was responsible for enforcing over 1,400 of them.

Food Rationing was the object of all this. It would begin in London and the South East. Colchester was quick off the mark. The mayor assembled the big guns, starting with Colchester's master of projects, Alderman Blaxill. Sugar rationing was introduced in December. All sugar retailers were registered and every household had to register with one of those retailers. Unsurprisingly, the Co-op was by far the most popular. Over 9,000 ration cards were then issued to all householders who had applied.

Blaxill extended this operation to cover Rhondda's list of weekly allowances: bread, 4lbs for women and 7lbs for men; meat, 1lb 8oz per person, half that for children under 6; sugar eight ounces; butter or margarine four ounces, each from a registered baker, butcher or grocer. Prices were set for these items and for milk by the Colchester Food

Control Committee. Inevitably local wholesalers and retailers claimed they were being robbed. Milk producers were particularly angry. Food shops had had an increasingly difficult war, compelled by staff shortages to introduce a one-and-a-half-hour lunchtime closure, compelled by DORA to shut at 6 pm, far earlier than was then normal, and now they were losing control over pricing.

Alderman Blaxill divided Colchester into ninety-six districts, corresponding with the existing national registration districts. All the borough's elementary schools were then closed for two days and all the 130 teachers sat at tables in the Moot Hall ready to handwrite 45,000 ration cards, which would then be hand delivered to all 10,000 households by boy scouts, who must have known their way round by now.

But the official cards did not arrive. The mayor rushed to London by train to find that government printing plans were in a mess. There were no cards. A speculative taxi ride to the government's printing plant revealed parcels of 10,000 cards addressed to London suburbs. A parcel was snatched and a triumphant mayor returned to Colchester. Working late, the exercise was completed on time and repeated all over again in June 1918 when additional items were rationed and ration books replaced ration cards. But rationing worked. It was even-handed and was seen to be fair. Very quickly the queues in Colchester disappeared.

This was just as well, for 1918 was going to be for Colchester a rollercoaster year.

Local schoolteachers camped in the Moot Hall handwriting the ration cards for Colchester.

CHAPTER 8

1918: Steadfast but Weary

As 1918 dawned there was not a lot to cheer in Colchester. The horrors of Passchendaele, the 'big push' of 1917, had only seemed to repeat the tactics of the Somme, with the same harvest of Colchester deaths. Though America had entered the war, Bolshevik Russia, with or without Paxman's aid, was suing for peace, enabling Germany to concentrate its forces on the Western Front. The end of the war seemed as far away as ever. Shortages were now serious, leading, as we have just seen, to margarine rebellion and full-scale rationing. Black Market activity is evident from several police prosecutions of soldiers stealing from army stores. A winter freeze caused a hundred burst pipes in a day and leaks so extensive that Jumbo the water tower pumped dry. Then heavy rain caused the river to flood.

On the first Sunday of the New Year, by proclamation of the King (but in practice the Archbishop of Canterbury), a National Day of Intercession was held with special services in all the churches and a great gathering of officialdom at St. Peter's, Colchester's civic church. It highlights the central role of formal religion in Britain's war, which was particularly marked in Colchester. The previous three years had been full of similar events. Following the initial Day of Prayer in August 1914, further Days of Prayer were held on the first Sunday of each year and every August to mark the anniversary of the outbreak of war.

FORMS

OF

PRAYER and THANKSGIVING

TO

ALMIGHTY GOD

TO BE USED ON

THE FEAST OF THE EPIPHANY
SUNDAY, THE SIXTH OF JANUARY, 1918

Being the Day appointed for Intercession on Behalf of the Nation and Empire in this Time of War.

Issued under the Authority of the Archbishops of Canterbury and York.

THE KING'S PROCLAMATION

¶ *In the Order of Holy Communion after the Creed at least once in the day, and at Morning or Evening Prayer, or before the Forms of Prayer hereinafter set forth, the Minister shall read the King's Proclamation, saying as follows:*

Brethren, I bid you hear the words of His Majesty the King appointing this day to be set aside as a Day of Prayer and Thanksgiving in all the Churches throughout his Dominions.

TO MY PEOPLE.—The world-wide struggle for the triumph of right and liberty is entering upon its last and most difficult phase. The enemy is striving by desperate assault and subtle intrigue to perpetuate the wrongs already committed and stem the tide of a free civilization. We have yet to complete the great task to which, more than three years ago, we dedicated ourselves.

At such a time I would call upon you to devote a special day to prayer that we may have the clear-sightedness and strength necessary to the victory of our cause. This victory will be gained only if we steadfastly remember the responsibility which rests upon us, and in a spirit of reverent obedience ask the blessing of Almighty God upon our endeavours. With hearts grateful for the Divine guidance which has led us so far towards our goal, let us seek to be enlightened in our understanding and fortified in our courage in facing the sacrifices we may yet have to make before our work is done.

I therefore hereby appoint January 6th—the first Sunday of the year—to be set aside as a special day of prayer and thanksgiving in all the Churches throughout my dominions, and require that this Proclamation be read at the services held on that day.

GEORGE R.I.

The official Proclamation for the National Day of Intercession in January 1918.

The response in Colchester was always considerable. Individual churches would be open all Sunday, with relays of services and continuous prayer sessions. In 1916 the two days prior to the first

Formal open-air worship had a long military tradition, as in this pre-war drumhead service in the cavalry barracks.

Sunday of the New Year were devoted to prayer and fasting. On the Saturday three Anglican churches were kept open all day and night for relays of volunteers to fill thirty-minute slots, maintaining twenty-four hours of continuous public prayer for victory and for those in the armed forces.

The August Days of Prayer were usually large open-air events such as one in 1915 on Abbey Field as part of a massive parade service and another at Castle Park in 1916 before the mayor and corporation, attended by thousands, which took place as families were losing sons, fathers and husbands at the Battle of the Somme. Clearly the act answered some need and pioneered the Remembrance Day services enacted every November at War Memorials ever since. The Castle Park service of August 1918, was also a combined event for Anglicans and Nonconformist (though not Roman Catholics) in which both sets of clergy took part. This alone makes these significant in the history of Colchester.

Colchester's Anglicans went further. They held a service of intercession at 12.30 pm every day at Holy Trinity Church until the war ended which any passer-by could attend. Initially, it was announced by the church bell but when the town acquired its air raid siren and its daily test was timed to 12.30, that took over the job. In addition, each

"Lift up your heads, for your redemption draweth nigh!"

FOURTH

ANNIVERSARY OF THE GREAT WAR.

COLCHESTER CITIZENS'

Commemoration Service

CASTLE PARK, 3 p.m., AUGUST 4th, 1918.

Hymn:

O GOD, our help in ages past,
　Our hope for years to come,
Our shelter from the stormy blast,
　And our eternal home;

Beneath the shadow of Thy Throne
　Thy saints have dwelt secure;
Sufficient is Thine Arm alone,
　And our defence is sure.

Time, like an ever-rolling stream,
　Bears all its sons away;
They fly forgotten, as a dream
　Dies at the opening day.

O God, our help in ages past,
　Our hope for years to come,
Be Thou our guard while troubles last,
　And our eternal home.　Amen.

The official programme for the 1918 anniversary service in Castle Park.

parish held its own service of intercession one evening a week. Increasingly this involved the reading out of names of members of that parish killed or missing and prayers for the dead, something of an innovation in Protestant tradition. The Anglo-Catholic vicar of St James on East Hill even set up three street shrines, complete with crosses, such as soldiers might see in Catholic France.

Nonconformist churches also held war-related prayer meetings within their regular devotional cycle. The churches thus served as a focus for war concerns: grief, anxiety, resolve; and Christianity was an essential arm of wartime social cohesion, notwithstanding the divide between the Church of England and the Nonconformist denominations. It was the clergy who compiled rolls of honour and would later erect war memorials.

As the war dragged on a new note marked the churches' response to war. In 1916 the Church of England launched an ambitious National Mission of Repentance and Hope. Inevitably it also tapped into that subconscious fear that with victory as far away as ever, God was angry with the sins of the church and the nation, which were ascribed to a pursuit of materialism or a lukewarm religious faith. In Colchester the mission was a major exercise, involving a personal letter from the Bishop of Chelmsford to every single household, and focused devotional activities in every church. The churches' failure to reach the working class was a common theme, though it seems unlikely that the mission changed that. That it took place at all was its most significant feature, for Anglicanism as the official church reached almost all citizens in some way.

Most Colchester residents would know which parish they lived in and the name of the vicar. They would be married in church; their babies

From Salvation Army bands to this funeral procession of clergy up Mersea Road, religion kept a visible presence in Colchester.

would be christened. Young boys were recruited for the parish choir; Sunday schools gave parents with large families a brief time to themselves, with the Sunday school's summer outing an incentive to keep up attendances. Many would encounter the parish structure via its charitable endeavours or system of district visitors. These had a good knowledge of local hardship, of problem families, of those with husbands or sons in the armed forces. The church might thus be the first port of call if bad news arrived, and there is good evidence that the churches carefully monitored members of their congregations in the forces.

Attendance at church on Sundays during the war was a more complex matter, though numbers appear to have risen. Traditionally Anglican congregations are at their largest at Christmas and at Easter Communion. Figures compiled by the historian Dr Robert Beaken show just under 2,500 Easter communicants for most of the war years against an adult civilian population of about 27-30,000. Some of those communicants would have been soldiers. Consistent Anglican Church going thus involved less than 10 per cent of the town. Nonconformist church membership was unlikely to have been more than 1,600, but numbers attending their churches at some stage would, if we include Roman Catholics, equal 2,500.

If, on average, 20 per cent of the town attended Sunday church, it was more like 80 per cent among the better off, as the affluent parish of St Mary's-at-the-Wall (now the Arts Centre), which served Lexden Road, demonstrated. But Colchester was also a town with a large social middle-class and here church going, if not every Sunday, was still common. Among the poor, regular church going was less likely, but certainly not absent. Here Nonconformist chapels were often more successful. Their Sunday Schools were larger, the most established having several hundred pupils; their evangelising efforts were more extensive, with the larger Nonconformist churches financing and staffing missions in various parts of the borough; and their more informal Sunday services were more accessible. This was recognised by the Anglicans and individual clergy gradually introduced more simplified services, notably for the church parades which they were soon providing, given the inability of the military to accommodate all soldiers under training in the Garrison Church.

The denominational divide was sharpened by the fact that Anglicans largely voted Conservative and Nonconformists Liberal. Lion Walk

Congregational Church, for example, supplied a string of Liberal councillors and mayors. A generation earlier the divisions had been bitter; now there was peaceful co-existence, a process which the shared trauma of war helped consolidate. From 1914 to 1918 Colchester's clergy and ministers were prominent, overworked figures. Torn by their own exclusion from military service, burdened with additional work as garrison and hospital chaplains, they had a tough war, several suffering from exhaustion and burnout during 1918.

By April 1918 Britain faced a military crisis. In yet another gamble, Germany launched a massive offensive, seeking to win the war before American troops arrived in Europe. Suddenly the Allies were in retreat. Passchendaele fell as they were driven back, across territory they had won, to the very banks of the Somme. The prospect of losing the war suddenly became real. The response of Colchester was to hold a public rally, complete with rousing speeches by the great and the good, asserting the town's commitment to the task. It was a view shared across the classes, as once more the possibility of invasion surfaced.

THE GERMAN OFFENSIVE

Harry Salmon, born 1895

..we went to Ypres; up on the Menin Road. That was a rough place. I remember being up to my neck in mud... couldn't get it off for days. It was not very nice, not very nice.... And the Germans were giving us hell. Shells were dropping all around us and they broke through on the left and the right of us. They swallowed up nearly all of our division and the order came through to 'get out as fast as you can'... And we got out – I don't know how I kept my crowd together really. And as we were retreating you had to keep going through a barrage of shells; some [of us] got through, some didn't. Old Jerry knew we were going like that and he put the shells down in front of us. That went on quite a while till we were all demoralised.... We didn't know where we were for days, but we eventually got through to Picquigny [on the Somme].

Alarming directives reached the mayor from London: 'Colchester citizens must nerve themselves for great sacrifice, her ambulances and

A meeting of the Brotherhood in Headgate Chapel shows the large numbers that such groups could muster.

special constabulary must convey the sick and helpless to a safer haven.... Evacuate the civil population and, if the grave hour ever comes, let the enemy find Colchester a barren desert.' The town's MP, Worthington Evans, now held the government post of Minister of Blockade. Invited to a meeting of the Nonconformist men's group, the Suffolk and Essex Brotherhood, he sent what must rank as one of the more unusual apologies for absence from a government minister:

> *The crisis is upon us! A crisis in which brute force is seeking to dominate the world. In order to foil this sinister attempt, the Empire is asking complete and ungrudging sacrifice, grim determination and continued confidence from its citizens. Faith and endurance is demanded from those at home. I hope your meeting is really and fully successful.*

As we now know, the crisis passed. By August it was Germany that was in retreat, but already the year had taken a heavy toll in British casualties. Trainloads of wounded arrived at Colchester and the local papers could scarcely keep pace with printing the photos of the young men who had died. Serious coal shortages meant households were now rationed, based on the number of rooms in a property. As Colchester's Fuel Control Committee realised, this was a blunt instrument, particularly unfair to the many poor who lived in various forms of shared households. Local knowledge, notably from Councillor Pat Green, was applied to make things fairer. This however did not prevent significant pilfering from the coal yards at the Hythe.

Laming Worthington Evans, Colchester's MP

Wartime inflation, something unknown before, was now eroding the benefits of full employment. Colchester's many small landlords, owners of just a few properties, found their rent income no longer paid the bills, and military billeting was on the decline. Inflation also roused the town's growing trade union movement, notably among public sector workers. Its more vocal elements, aware of the dramatic events in Russia, were already proclaiming that they offered workers a more satisfactory religion: socialism.

In the midst of these testing times, Colchester's overstretched garrison was playing a key part in understanding what we now call post-traumatic stress disorder (PTSD) From the American Civil War to the Boer War large numbers of soldiers had been side-lined after battle and discharged from the Army with chest pains, palpitations or breathlessness. Described as 'soldier's heart' it became the subject of medical study from the 1860s. Heavy army kit, tight uniforms and repetitive drill routines were each in turn blamed, and it was only after 1906 that Dr Mackenzie, a heart specialist, was asked to do further research. He soon pointed out that the symptoms of soldier's heart could be found in the civilian workplace, and among the obese solely as a result of heavy exercise.

The outbreak of war in 1914 soon produced cases of soldier's heart among the British Expeditionary Force. By May 1918 the total discharged from the forces on pensions was over 41,000, most of them believing (incorrectly) that they had a defective heart. Dr Mackenzie pressed for the establishment of a special hospital for all those afflicted to establish cause. This was opened at Mount Vernon Hospital,

Sobraon Barracks.

Hampstead in 1916, but overwhelmed by numbers, the unit was transferred in October 1917 to Colchester where Sobraon Barracks was converted into a 700-bed hospital. Here patients were admitted at the rate of 150 a week. In charge was Dr Thomas Lewis, a brilliant researcher who after studying 1,000 cases, accepted that soldier's heart, which he re-named 'effort syndrome', was nothing to do with cardiac malfunction, but was the result of the stress and rigour of trench warfare.

The army was anxious on two scores. Firstly, it was keen to get the afflicted back into action as soon as possible. Hitherto, those discharged with soldier's heart had spent an average of five and a half months in hospital. Lewis built up a regime of carefully measured, graded exercises, based on standard army drill. Soon he had 500 men being drilled daily on the Sobraon parade ground, most of whom were returned to army duty within six weeks. Far fewer now needed to be discharged, reassuring the army on its second concern: the cost of future pensions to those discharged, who, as Lewis demonstrated, were not strictly physically ill at all. Lewis duly became, after the war, consultant physician to the Ministry of Pensions on disease of the heart, where the expertise built up at Colchester reduced the pensions bill from £106million to £63million. He also trained a new generation of doctors to identify the condition.

The success of the Colchester unit during 1918 attracted leading medical officers from the Canadian and US Armies, where soldiers' heart symptoms had been labelled 'neurocirculatory asthenia', to come to the Sobraon Hospital and work with the British experts and make

Specialist staff at the Colchester Heart Hospital. Sitting centre between the nursing sisters are three leading American heart doctors.

recommendations to their own medical high commands. Several of these Americans went on to become leaders in their field and modern cardiology was spearheaded by Anglo-American expertise. The work on soldier's heart also links to that more dramatic 1914-18 manifestation of PTSD, shellshock, a condition which was initially considered to be caused by a minor cerebral haemorrhage, but while taking other factors into account was increasingly recognised to be, like the Vietnam and Gulf War Syndromes would be later, psychiatric in origin. The beginning of government support of medical research, the recognition of PTSD, the training of the next generation of cardiologists, indeed the birth of modern cardiology, can thus trace roots back to Sobraon Barracks, Colchester.

While this significant research progressed, in early July Colchester's Acting Medical Officer of Health informed the borough council that 'a large number of military cases of 'flu, of a rather peculiar type, had been admitted to the isolation hospital'. In two days there had been fifty-five cases from the Military Hospital alone and 'similar cases were occurring in the town'. Soon it had a name, Spanish 'Flu, and it was rampant in the town. It hit all classes. The retiring mayor, Councillor Jarmin, lost his son, a Kitchener Volunteer, who had survived being gassed at Ypres. His young wife also died within days. The Colchester

Soldiers reverse arms ahead of the coffin of yet another military funeral, a familiar sight through four years of war.

During the flu epidemic the section set aside at Colchester Cemetery for the Military Hospital filled up rapidly. Along with the UK dead lay Canadians, Belgians and German prisoners of war.

press suggested it was killing more people than the war did. In fact, the 1918 'flu pandemic would kill at least 50 million, far, far more than the war. This was because about a third of mankind was affected and the virus was unprecedentedly virulent.

Latest research suggests that a human 'flu virus, active in the 1890s, was modified by a bird 'flu virus. People over 40 were protected by immunity gained from contracting earlier 'flu viruses, but those born after 1890 were terribly vulnerable. It thus hit the very age range from which much of the Army was drawn. Perhaps in consequence the Colchester epidemic actually accelerated when elsewhere in the UK it had already peaked. By November 1918 patients in the Military Hospital were dying from it at the rate of ten a day. Seventy local women came forward when the mayor asked for volunteers to help in the wards. Across Colchester the deaths for November alone were 162. Thousands more just got ill and were off work. Business could barely cope. Schools were particularly hit and were closed for six weeks. Cinemas and theatres were disinfected after every performance. When the epidemic subsided in 1919 it had killed 323 across Colchester.

In the midst of this crisis the war suddenly ended. Since October rumour in Colchester had held that a German collapse was imminent. Thus at the eleventh hour of the eleventh day.... we can all complete that sentence. The town council was actually in session when the Armistice was announced. They rose to their feet and sang the National Anthem, then trooped out onto the town hall balcony to face the crowd gathering below, for the Armistice was now an open secret. Three army buglers perched dangerously on a window sill and sounded the 'attention' before the mayor addressed the crowd:

Fellow citizens rejoice with me this day – the greatest day in the world's history. An armistice has been signed. Congratulate yourselves on this marvellous victory.... May we have a world peace and may all those waiting for their dear and loved ones have them soon returned...

Soon there were crowds everywhere, animated and excited. It was Monday and little work was done that week. Munition workers were given three days off and celebrations went on into the night. The

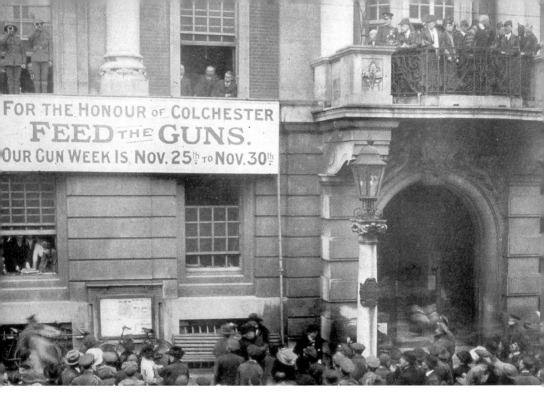

FOR THE HONOUR OF COLCHESTER
FEED THE GUNS.
OUR GUN WEEK IS NOV. 25th TO NOV. 30th

The mayor, George Wright, wearing his chain of office, announces the Armistice from the balcony of Colchester Town Hall. The large placard proclaims the latest fund-raising project in the town.

following day there was a procession of workers to the town hall, led by the Paxman brass band. The mayor and the workers' leaders made short speeches. The band played *Rule Britannia* and the procession set off round the town. The mood, the papers implied, was wholly celebratory, but the recollections of Gladys Hayhoe (below) show that some were already preparing for the next war: labour versus capital.

A civic Service of Thanksgiving, attended by thirty clergy, nonconformist ministers and Army chaplains, was held at St Peter's Church. About 1,000 people crammed in, 2,000 more were turned away and an 'overflow' service was arranged at the main Nonconformist Church, Lion Walk. The sermon at St Peter's was preached by Rev Kenneth Parry, minister of Lion Walk, the first time that a Nonconformist minister had preached in an Anglican pulpit in Colchester, while Rev. Harris of St Nicholas conducted the Lion Walk 'overflow'. Such a gesture appropriately caught the sense of a united and relieved Establishment.

THE ARMISTICE

Sidney Murrells, born 1892
When the Armistice was signed, people were dancing and shouting all over the place. They were walking up the High Street singing and dancing. They were putting fireworks and balloons up against the lampposts and the police never took any notice.

Mrs Bareham, born 1913
There was a lot of – er, jollification, but a lot of sadness. [pause].... *my father, when he came home, he was very tired and... for a long time, my mother was frightened to go up to bed 'cause he'd lash out* [in his sleep] *– 'cause of the war.*
'Did he ever talk about the war?'
Not a lot.

Gladys Hayhoe, born 1901
'What happened [at Paxman's] when the war ended?'
Oh, everything stopped! Someone to do with the union came round and asked us if we were going on the march round the town. Well, being young and excited, we said, 'Yes'. They all marched round town and ended up in St Botolph's Street [at the Independent Labour Party Office]... *and one man went upstairs to a room and he was inciting the people to strike really, and stand out for further wages or working hours.... The workmen were cheering, yes.... Course, they knew we* [women workers] *wouldn't last. And we had a month's notice. And then we were on the dole, of course.*

Though hostilities had ended it was agreed to go ahead with Colchester's 'Feed the Guns' week, scheduled for late November, the latest effort to persuade the town to lend their money to the government. Colchester's contributions to these occasional appeals had not been glorious, and regularly fell short of the town's population-based targets. Even when announced by leaflets dropped by aeroplane, itself a symbol of how far technology had advanced in four years of war, Colchester purchased war bonds or National Saving Certificates to the value of £193,367 against their £250,000 target, and a significant slice of that came via town council investments, for the interest rate was good.

December 1918 was dominated by the discussion of pay rises to public sector workers, granted, not always generously, the following month. There was also a general election campaign with an enlarged constituency and a much-enlarged electorate, which for the first time included women. It also, for the first time included a Labour candidate. Andrew Conley was the Deputy Secretary of the powerful United Garment Workers Union, an industry boasting seven factories in Colchester. Equally significantly, the Liberal party did not offer a candidate, an ominous sign of the party's uncertain future. Special arrangements were made to supply servicemen still in uniform with a postal vote. Indeed, Colchester's fluid population was reflected in the number of residents whose stay had been too short to gain the right of residence. This included sixteen nurses, all over 30, at the Sobraon Heart Hospital.

The class war preached by the Paxman trade unionists at the 'march round the town' was met in equal measure by the Conservative Party and its mouthpiece the *Essex County Standard* in the short election campaign. Despite Labour's very moderate agenda, they were regularly rubbished as Bolsheviks, against whom British troops were now fighting, and the *Standard* declared on the eve of poll that voting Labour was what the Huns, the unrepentant German nation, wanted voters to do.

With the irksome blackout over, the town was again lit up for Christmas 1918, except that one third of Colchester's street lights no longer worked properly. Every effort was made, despite the continued rationing, to make it feel like a pre-war Christmas, but gaps were everywhere: the dead in Flanders Field, those dead from Spanish 'Flu, the husbands, the sons still in France. As an orange, a new penny and some nuts went into a thousand children's stockings, in a town of fatherless children the best-selling toy in the shops was a model wartime tank.

At Christmas 1918 street and shop lights shone out again, highlighting the tram lines round Headgate Corner.

CHAPTER 9

Legacy

The Great War cast a long shadow across Colchester. It is easy to summarise. There was no land fit for heroes, indeed, very few homes for heroes, and no War To End All Wars – most people lived to see the next one. The full employment of wartime collapsed into depression. Colchester suffered unemployment as severe as the more publicised towns of the North and never recovered its Edwardian ebullience. Then there was the lost generation, the Glorious Dead, gathered, when they could be found, and reburied beneath row upon row of War Grave headstones. Theirs was the silent presence in Colchester. But life went

More active trade unionism marked post-war Colchester. This 1920 Workers Union demonstration was on behalf of agricultural workers.

on; people coped. The age of the stiff upper lip ensured that it is left to us to be appalled at the statistics of death and ask, *'how* did they cope?'

Calculating Colchester's contribution is not easy. We begin with the, approximately, 4,300 Colchester servicemen still abroad in December 1918, given a postal vote in the General Election. With the limited number of men demobilised by then, these must represent the bulk of those in the forces. To this we can add at least 1,250 who had died and, based on national statistics, perhaps 650 discharged from the forces with an injury which affected the rest of their life: loss of mobility, the effects of gas or wounds, PTSD or other psychiatric damage. This suggests an approximate 6,200 who fought in the war, half Colchester's adult male population.

The number of dead is also approximate, but telling. Though initially 1,263 names were gathered for Colchester's War Memorial, there are omissions, but additions too. The names were collected by the town hall, not taken from official figures and included men born in the town, whose families still lived here, but who themselves had left before 1914. Colchester's fluid wartime population also meant that the families of some of those killed had left the area before the list was compiled.

Colchester abounded with solemn war memorials remembering the dead. This is at the Colchester Royal Grammar School where almost 20 per cent of those who served died.

The figures imply a Colchester death rate of 20 per cent, similar to the figure for the ex-pupils of its Grammar School, but almost twice the national average of just over 11½ per cent. To this we can add the estimated 650 discharged with a disability, a figure that was likely to rise as time went by. This is a total and a percentage much higher than most other towns, partly from its all-inclusive approach and also because Colchester had a large middle class, where casualties were higher, and many men in the Territorials and Reserves, who, serving from the outset, were more likely to be killed.

Nor does it end there. Of those who saw conflict a significant number were likely to carry psychological scars, scars which most of them took to their grave. And it ran across the wider district. In 1919, of the 1,095 footballers registered in 1914 with the Essex & Suffolk Border League in which Colchester played, 480 had been killed. Of the Colchester Town team, seven had died. Small wonder that war cast so long a shadow; that the town erected so dramatic a War Memorial.

Hilda Riches, born 1901

I had 3 brothers that went. My brother Charlie went to Canada when he was 18 and he joined up with the Canadian forces. Bert had a bad shrapnel wound and Lawson had a bullet which went just past his windpipe; and when the surgeon took it out and gave it to him he said, 'you can keep that; you will never be nearer death than you have been'. So they both got wounded in the war.

They came home all right?

Yes; they came home OK, but Bert was rather queer for a long time, but he got over it. Because he lay between the English and German lines for so long and when he thought he would get up he was sort-of shelled and he had several bits of nasty shrapnel in his back.

Sonny Cracknell, born 1901

Me uncle Fred he was called up and within two months he was dead. And he left two young boys.

Gwen Mason, born 1923

[As a child] *I was really frightened of 'Shellshock'. He used to walk about and shout. I could tell the grown-ups were frightened of him and got out the way. People would see him coming and shout 'Shellshock!'...*
There was another man like him down Pownall Crescent.

The town wound down slowly from its war footing. Rationing and price controls continued. It was well into 1919 before, one by one, the many busy organisations set up to cater for troops held their last meeting and balanced their books. Red Cross Hospitals handed out honours to key staff and surrendered their premises to former owners. Up on the Abbey Field it was strangely quiet and 'an unholy mess'. Heavy artillery and constant transport had battered the roads; muddy puddles peppered the once green fields, beaten bare by constant training exercises. Discarded stores piled high; unwanted artillery,

The official Victory Parade around Colchester travelling down St Botolph's Street.

A rare aerial view of the long winding trail of the July Victory Parade.

buckets and wheelbarrows lay rusting. Rats romped in discarded fodder. Those needing housing looked with envy on row upon row of empty wooden huts. The army's solution was to auction everything off over 1919-20: spades, wheelbarrows, huts, beds, motorbikes, lorries, wagons, field ovens. Quantities could be prodigious: 20,000 pickaxe heads, 6,800 six-foot tables and 4,800 bicycles, for example. The local fishing industry was less pleased to have hundreds of tons of surplus ammunition dumped in the river estuary.

A Victory Celebration Week was organised in July. A united service in Castle Park and a 1,500-strong procession of civic and military leaders attracted hundreds. On Victory Day garrison troops and a naval detachment marched round Colchester, hung for the occasion with bunting and Union Jacks, to assemble in front of the town hall alongside a detachment of citizen soldiers, demobilised and dressed in civilian clothes. A Grand Free Fete followed on Abbey Field and an

Uniformed and discharged servicemen stand side by side under a sober banner at the High Street Victory Parade.

athletics contest on Paxman's Sports Ground at Land Lane. In the evening music was played in Castle Park as fireworks and a bonfire concluded the celebration. Later that week over 6,000 children sat down to a 'peace treat' on the Old Heath Recreation Ground.

Such cheerfulness did not dispel the grim reality of rising unemployment, which set in after a brief post-war boom. It was matched by a rising trade union presence and class bitterness. In September there was a national rail strike and a national strike of foundrymen. This seriously hit Colchester's engineering firms when in loyalty to the union the men stayed out on strike even after voting as a branch to resume work. In May, the registered unemployment rate in Colchester was 666; by January 1920 it was 1,684 rising to 2,282 in 1921 and 2,844 in 1922. That was a civilian unemployment rate of 17 per cent overall in the town and about 20 per cent among men.

Half of these were ex-servicemen, who adopted a vocal opposition to those relatively few women who had retained jobs historically done by men. Queues at the Labour Exchange grew longer. The Council eventually secured some government funding to provide paid labouring for unemployed men, consolidating quays at the Hythe against hoped-for future trade. It was rough work. Colchester was also one of only eleven towns to set up (in Magdalen Street) a branch of Lord Roberts Memorial Workshops to provide employment for wounded ex-servicemen, making baskets and various kinds of furniture.

Unemployed men set to work consolidating the stone quays on the River Colne.

Colchester was one of a handful of towns establishing a Lord Roberts Workshop to provided work for injured ex-servicemen.

Despite the best of intentions, the Council made slow progress building the 800 new homes they envisaged: Colchester's first council houses. The first nine were not ready for occupation until 1921. High construction costs made an economic rent impossible. Private builders condemned a scheme, which soon fell victim to government cuts. Nor, as 1922 ended, did Colchester yet have a civic War Memorial, despite the Council having established a War Memorial Committee before the Armistice. Other memorials abounded: in churches, in workplaces, in Friendly Society halls, at the garrison, at the grammar school – some thirty-one in all.

It had been the ubiquitous Gurney Benham who had persuaded the borough committee to fund a practical memorial: a war museum and the transformation of the Albert School into an art gallery. To this was later added a memorial block at the hospital. Benham was a gifted artist and was anxious to find a home for the collection of local watercolours, which his mother, who had recently died, had left. Benham, a Conservative, was joined by Wilson Marriage, a Liberal. He then recruited James Paxman, Colchester's most munificent patron, now retired and living in Bournemouth. Thus was reassembled the trio who had conceived and built the new town hall.

Memorial: this tank, presented to Colchester after the war, sat on a plinth in Castle Park, replacing a Boer War cannon.

But for once Benham had misread the town. On Christmas Day 1918 Dr Hunt, the GP husband of Dame Catherine Hunt, wrote to the *Essex County Standard* a deeply emotional letter:

> *Now, ... before any other consideration, what should a war memorial be? It should be something obviously erected to the memory of those who have fallen in the Great War... a mark of love for and gratitude to those who had made the sacrifice than which there is none greater, an object lesson of their devotion to duty... of their patriotism – a tangible proof of what this generation did at a great crisis in our history and an example and an incentive to future generations. ...*
>
> *Remember the ground on which our memorial is erected will be holy ground. Alas! we cannot visit the last resting place of all our fallen in the various battlefields.... [but] We could visit on one day annually (perhaps the best day would be the Sunday nearest Armistice Day) our war memorial for a suitable service,*

*when a wreath from the Corporation could be placed on a noble
group of sculpture... representing Victory and Peace, the triumph
of Right over Might... erected in the High Street.*

*Our beloved fallen took up their cross under the banner of
Christ, and fought and fell in the greatest crusade in the world's
history... I am writing this on Christmas Day, the most
memorable Christmas since the first* [Christmas]. *A great thank
offering to God is due from Colchester.*

Hunt's letter was one of the most fruitful ever
written to a Colchester newspaper. It spelt out
almost exactly what did happen, even as it rejected
exploiting the war to provide something like an art
gallery. It took time to get agreement via a public
meeting of the town setting up a public War
Memorial Committee of leading citizens, before a
suitable compromise was reached between a sacred
memorial and a useful project. There would be 'a
sculptured monument' to cost no more than £3,000.
Any further money raised would be used to build a
memorial block at the Essex County Hospital.

Unsurprisingly there was a generous response: *Dr Edgar Hunt, godfather*
£7,600 was raised from individual contributions, an *of Colchester's War*
economic value of £2.5 million in 2016. *Memorial.*

A gesture now came from Lord Cowdray, one of
the richest men in England, and Colchester's MP prior to 1910. He
purchased both the Castle and Holly Trees house with its twenty-seven
acres of parkland from the Round family as his memorial, to be
integrated into Castle Park. Working with Duncan Clark, the leading
architect in the district, he then bought and demolished the marble
works of Lent Watts which stood beside it, opening out a view of the
Castle where an ornamental crescent, Cowdray Crescent, designed by
Clark, provided a setting for a Cenotaph War Memorial, with the view
behind it of the Norman Castle, speaking of Colchester's long history.

A leading sculptor of war memorials, Henry Fehr, produced the
memorial we see today. Above it soars a winged Angel of Victory,
bearing a sword and a victor's wreath, a symbolic figure Fehr placed
on at least eight other war memorials. Below were larger than life size

sculptures of St George in full medieval armour and a helmeted statue of Peace, holding a dove aloft. Though they did not know it, the memorial stood above the arcade of Britain's most important Roman temple. In the memorial's base was placed a time capsule of contemporary medals, newspapers, directories, tram timetables, and, most notably, a handwritten list of 1,248 people known for certain to have died as a result of the conflict. It included one women, Sybil Stanford, a Red Cross nurse who died of Spanish 'Flu, and a teenager, Geoffrey Barnes, who had just left school, killed when the ship he was travelling in was sunk by a German mine. A duplicate list hangs in the town hall.

Together, the wording of Hunt's letter and the memorial's design make clear how the war was now seen, at least by Colchester's articulate classes. There was no statue of a contemporary soldier, no hint of mud or mutilation, let alone a blood bath, only symbolism: swords not guns, 'fallen' not dead; a medieval knight recalling chivalry and crusade; men fighting 'under the banner of Christ', serving King and Country with 'patriotism' and 'duty', an angel offering Heavenly reward. The message was firm: so much death had not been in vain. Right had defeated Might; civilisation had been saved.

While this noble concept was upheld, more mundane consequences of war occupied some survivors. Military life had led to a worrying spread of venereal disease. A week after the Armistice Colchester's main cinema began to show the 'magnificently broad minded' information film *Open Your Eyes* to large audiences, a topic and an approach which would have been inconceivable four years earlier. Other films on the same subject appeared the following year as with the arrival of ragtime (jazz), cultural change was afoot. Deference would never be quite the same again.

With all its considerable logistics, it was May 1923, a late date for such an event, before the official unveiling of Colchester's civic war memorial by the army's most senior officer, Field Marshal Sir William Robertson. Dr Hunt himself had now died. After the dedication the relatives of the dead were permitted to move closer to the memorial for the official opening. As the rather clumsy covering fell aside, there was a visible surge towards the cenotaph, as if to touch it. Mothers, wives, families needed closure, though many only achieved this by a visit to the war graves of France much later.

PROGRAMME
for

WEEK COMMENCING MONDAY, NOVEMBER 21st.

EXTRA : SPECIAL : WEEK.

MONDAY TO WEDNESDAY.

The Latest Achievement in Propaganda Films!

OPEN · YOUR · EYES.

Magnificently broadminded. A wonderful treatise upon social and sex problems, containing a definite trend toward a finer moral inspiration; illustrating the tragedies resulting from the so-called double standard of morality. Into the main theme have been woven supplementary incidents, each drawn FROM ACTUAL LIFE—calculated to make a direct appeal to EVERYONE in the audience; told in the most healthy manner possible.

The trend nowadays is towards a finer philosophy of life.
We cannot have an A1 nation with C3 ideas.
The whole fundamental idea is to open your eyes.

FOR ADULTS ONLY! No Person under 16 admitted.

FULL SELECT PROGRAMME.

THURSDAY TO SATURDAY.

F. Brooke-Warren's world-famous Melodrama,

THE FACE AT THE WINDOW.

The play that has run for more than twenty years.

FULL SELECT PROGRAMME.

NON-STOP
PROGRAMME

**THE HEADGATE
ELECTRIC THEATRE,**
COLCHESTER.   [716

As the soldiers came home, Open Your Eyes, *a film dealing with venereal disease, ran to large houses in Colchester.*

The moment after the unveiling of Colchester's civic war memorial when relatives of the dead surged towards the memorial.

The official dedication of Tiptree's British Legion colours.

With Colchester's War Memorial came a lavish commemorative booklet. Like much First World War literature it was full of purple prose, bursting with superlatives. It is as if a generation were determined to persuade us of the exceptionalism of what they had gone through. One recalls the mayor of Colchester at the Armistice announcing 'the greatest day in the world's history,' or the Bishop of Colchester calling the war 'the most stupendous in the history of the civilised world'. Even that measured observer, Gurney Benham, described 1918 as 'probably the most dramatic and fateful in the history of the civilised world'. When it came to writing the memorial booklet the editor, himself a wartime mayor, was anxious that future generations should know 'what happened in those four stupendous and strenuous years.'

For the men who came home less articulate, their comfort came from meeting fellow soldiers in the camaraderie and reunions of the British Legion and the Comrades of the Great War. And once a year, as we still do, they gathered on the Sunday nearest Armistice Day to sound the Last Post and proclaim that 'at the going down of the sun and in the morning we will remember them'.

One hundred years on, the Great War's long shadow is with Colchester still.

A newspaper photo of the crowd of 20,000 attending a British Legion Rally in Colchester's Castle Park.

Index